AA

Cycle Rides

D0513255

London
& the South Coast

Publisher: David Watchus
Managing Editor: Isla Love
Senior Editor: Donna Wood
Senior Designer: Kat Mead
Picture Research: Lesley Grayson
Cartographic Editor: Geoff Chapman
Cartographic Production: Anna Thompson

Produced by AA Publishing
© Automobile Association Developments Limited 2007

Published by AA Publishing (a trading name of Automobile Association Developments Limited, whose registered office is Fanum House, Basing View, Basingstoke, Hampshire RG21 4EA; registered number 1878835).

 This product includes mapping data licensed from the Ordnance Survey® with the permission of the Controller of Her Majesty's Stationery Office. © Crown copyright 2007. All rights reserved. Licence number 100021153.

A03033c

ISBN-10: 0-7495-5191-7
ISBN-13: 978-0-7495-5191-9

A CIP catalogue record for this book is available from the British Library.

The contents of this book are believed correct at the time of printing. Nevertheless, the publishers cannot be held responsible for any errors or omissions or for changes in the details given in this book or for the consequences of any reliance on the information it provides. We have tried to ensure accuracy in this book, but things do change and we would be grateful if readers could advise us of any inaccuracies they may encounter. This does not affect your statutory rights.

We have taken all reasonable steps to ensure that the cycle rides in this book are safe and achievable by people with a reasonable level of fitness. However, all outdoor activities involve a degree of risk and the publishers accept no responsibility for any injuries caused to readers whilst following these cycle rides. For advice on cycling in safety, see pages 10–11.

Some of the cycle rides may appear in other AA books and publications.

Visit AA Publishing's website www.theAA.com/travel

Colour reproduction by Keene Group, Andover
Printed in Italy by G Canale & C SPA

Cycle Rides

London & the South Coast

Contents

Locator map

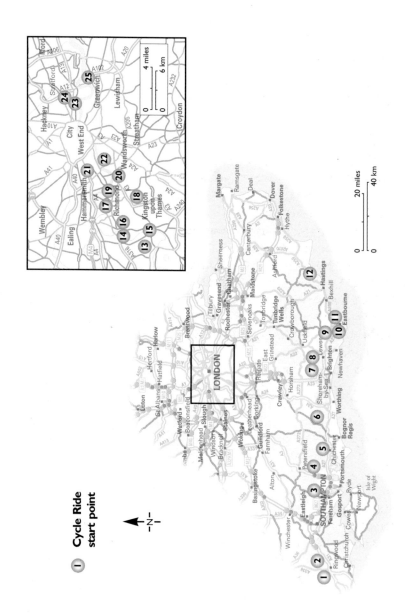

Cycle Ride
start point

Introduction to London & the South Coast

This guide includes a surprising variety of cycle rides in London and on its outskirts, easily accessible from the city, as well as a good selection from the neighbouring counties of Hampshire, Surrey, and East and West Sussex. In the capital, there are routes in central areas such as Putney, Fulham, and Greenwich, as well as some lovely traffic-free routes through the city's parks including Hyde Park and Battersea Park. If the centre of town isn't for you, you could try the cycle ride around one of Europe's largest city parks, Richmond Park, or the route through Wimbledon Common.

In this region, one of the most popular with tourists in the whole of Britain, there are limitless places to visit, either along the way or once you have finished your ride. Attractions include grand houses and immaculate palaces, some managed by English Heritage or The National Trust. As you might expect, several routes follow the River Thames. You can cycle along the river from attractive towns to impressive houses by going from Richmond to Ham House or from Kingston-upon-Thames to Hampton Court. Other cycle rides take you alongside canals, such as the ride along Regent's

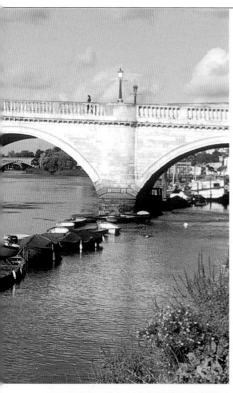

Canal, and many routes in and around the city provide a welcome opportunity to escape to open, green spaces, such as Bushy Park, where you can spot wildlife or enjoy gardens.

The cycle rides in East and West Sussex take in Roman sites such as the Bignor Roman Villa, wartime defences and the chance to enjoy spectacular views over the South Downs to the lively and bustling city of Brighton. The Cuckoo Trail around Hailsham traverses a cycle-friendly route along a railway track through peaceful countryside to reach Michelham Priory. Other rides in this book take you to the historic towns of Rye and Winchelsea and pass close to the sandy beaches for which the region is well known.

In Hampshire, the wooded glades of the New Forest are always popular with cyclists, particularly family groups, and there is a chance to explore the Queen Elizabeth Country Park or the lovely Meon Valley.

Left: The bridge over the Thames at Richmond
Below: Relaxing in Regent's Park

Using this book

SHORTER ALTERNATIVE ROUTE

Each cycle ride has a panel giving essential information for the cyclist, including the distance, terrain, nature of the paths, nearest public toilets and cycle hire.

2 **MAP:** OS Explorer OL24 White Peak

START/FINISH: Rudyard Old Station, grid ref
3 SJ955579

TRAILS/TRACKS: old railway trackbed

LANDSCAPE: wooded lake shore, peaceful pastures and meadows

PUBLIC TOILETS: Rudyard village

5 **TOURIST INFORMATION:** Leek, tel 01538 483741

6 **CYCLE HIRE:** none near by

THE PUB: The Abbey Inn, Leek, see 'Directions'

7 ❶ Take care along the banks of the lake – keep well away from the shore line

---

1 **MINIMUM TIME:** The time stated for completing each ride is the estimated minimum time that a reasonably fit family group of cyclists would take to complete the circuit. This does not allow for rest or refreshment stops.

2 **MAPS:** Each route is shown on a detailed map. However, some detail is lost because of the restrictions imposed by scale, so for this reason, we recommend that you use the maps in conjunction with a more detailed Ordnance Survey map. The relevant Ordnance Survey Explorer map appropriate for each cycle is listed.

3 **START/FINISH:** Here we indicate the start location and parking area. There is a six-figure grid reference prefixed by two letters showing which 100km square of the National Grid it refers to. You'll find more information on grid references on most Ordnance Survey maps.

4 **LEVEL OF DIFFICULTY:** The cycle rides have been graded simply (1 to 3) to give an indication of their relative difficulty. Easier routes, such as those with little total ascent, on easy level trails, or those covering shorter distances are graded 1. The hardest routes, either because they include a lot of ascent, greater distances,

or are across hilly, more demanding terrains, are graded 3.

5 **TOURIST INFORMATION:** The nearest tourist information office and contact number is given for further local information, in particular opening details for the attractions listed in the 'Where to go from here' section.

6 **CYCLE HIRE:** We list, within reason, the nearest cycle hire shop/centre.

7 ❶ Here we highlight any potential difficulties or dangers along the route. At a glance you will know if a route is steep or crosses difficult terrain, or if a cycle ride is hilly, encounters a main road, or whether a mountain bike is essential for the off-road trails. If we feel that a particular cycle route is only suitable for older, fitter children we say so here.

About the pubs

Generally, all the pubs featured are on the cycle route. Some are close to the start/finish point, others are at the midway point, and occasionally, the recommended pub is a short drive from the start/finish point. We have included a cross-section of pubs, from homely village locals and isolated rural gems to traditional inns and upmarket country pubs which specialise in food. What they all have in common is that they serve food and welcome children.

The description of the pub is intended to convey its history and character and in the 'food' section we list a selection of dishes, which indicate the style of food available. Under 'family facilities', we say if the pub offers a children's menu or smaller portions of adult dishes, and whether the pub has a family room, high chairs, baby-changing facilities, or toys. There is detail on the garden, terrace, and any play area.

DIRECTIONS: If the pub is very close to the start point we say see Getting to the Start. If the pub is on the route the relevant direction/map location number is given, in addition to general directions. In some cases the pub is a short drive away from the finish point, so we give detailed directions to the pub from the end of the route.

PARKING: The number of parking spaces is given. All but a few of the rides start away from the pub. If the pub car park is the parking/start point, then we have been given permission by the landlord to print the fact. You should always let the landlord or a member of staff know that you are using the car park before setting off.

OPEN: If the pub is open all week we state 'daily' and if it's open throughout the day we say 'all day', otherwise we just give the days/sessions the pub is closed.

FOOD: If the pub serves food all week we state 'daily' and if food is served throughout the day we say 'all day', otherwise we just give the days/sessions when food is not served.

BREWERY/COMPANY: This is the name of the brewery to which the pub is tied or the pub company that owns it. 'Free house' means that the pub is independently owned and run.

REAL ALE: We list the regular real ales available on handpump. 'Guest beers' indicates that the pub rotates beers from a number of microbreweries.

ROOMS: We list the number of bedrooms and how many are en suite. For prices please call the pub.

Please note that pubs change hands frequently and new chefs are employed, so menu details and facilities may change at short notice. Not all the pubs featured in this guide are listed in the *AA Pub Guide*. For information on those that are, including AA-rated accommodation, and for a comprehensive selection of pubs across Britain, please refer to the *AA Pub Guide* or see the AA's website www.theAA.com

Alternative refreshment stops
At a glance you will see if there are other pubs or cafés along the route. If there are no other places on the route, we list the nearest village or town where you can find somewhere else to eat and drink.

☛ Where to go from here
Many of the routes are short and may only take a few hours. You may wish to explore part of the surrounding area after lunch or before tackling the route, so we have selected a few nearby attractions with children in mind.

9

Cycling in safety

CYCLING

Cycling is a fun activity which children love, and teaching your child to ride a bike and going on family cycling trips are rewarding experiences. Not only is cycling a great way to travel, but as a regular form of exercise it can make an invaluable contribution to a child's health and fitness, and increase their confidence and sense of independence.

However, the growth of motor traffic has made Britain's roads increasingly dangerous and unattractive to cyclists. Cycling with children is an added responsibility and, as with everything, there is a risk when taking them out for a day's cycling. In recent years many measures have been taken to address this, including the on-going development of the National Cycle Network (8,000 miles utilising quiet lanes and traffic-free paths) and local designated off-road routes for families, such as converted railway lines, canal towpaths and forest tracks.

In devising the cycle rides in this guide, every effort has been made to use these designated cycle paths, or to link them with quiet country lanes and waymarked byways and bridleways. Unavoidably, in a few cases, some relatively busy B-roads have been used to link the quieter, more attractive routes.

Rules of the road
- Ride in single file on narrow and busy roads.
- Be alert, look and listen for traffic, especially on narrow lanes and blind bends and be extra careful when descending steep hills, as loose gravel can lead to an accident.
- In wet weather make sure you keep a good distance between you and other riders.
- Make sure you indicate your intentions clearly.
- Brush up on *The Highway Code* before venturing out on to the road.

Off-road safety code of conduct
- Only ride where you know it is legal to do so. It is forbidden to cycle on public footpaths, marked in yellow. The only 'rights of way' open to cyclists are bridleways (blue markers) and unsurfaced tracks, known as byways, which are open to all traffic and waymarked in red.
- Canal towpaths: you need a permit to cycle on some stretches of towpath (www.waterscape.com). Remember that access paths can be steep and slippery and always get off and push your bike under low bridges and by locks.
- Always yield to walkers and horses, giving adequate warning of your approach.
- Don't expect to cycle at high speeds.
- Keep to the main trail to avoid any unnecessary erosion to the area beside the trail and to prevent skidding, especially if it is wet.
- Remember the Country Code.

Cycling with children
Children can use a child seat from the age of eight months, or from the time they can hold themselves upright. There are a number of child seats available which fit on the front or rear of a bike and towable two-seat trailers are worth investigating. 'Trailer bicycles', suitable for five- to ten-

year-olds, can be attached to the rear of an adult's bike, so that the adult has control, allowing the child to pedal if he/she wishes. Family cycling can be made easier by using a tandem, as it can carry a child seat and tow trailers. 'Kiddy-cranks' for shorter legs can be fitted to the rear seat tube, enabling either parent to take their child out cycling. With older children it is better to purchase the right size bike rather than one that is too big, as an oversized bike will be difficult to control, and potentially dangerous.

Preparing your bicycle

A basic routine includes checking the wheels for broken spokes or excess play in the bearings, and checking the tyres for punctures, undue wear and the correct tyre pressures. Ensure that the brake blocks are firmly in place and not worn, and that cables are not frayed or too slack. Lubricate hubs, pedals, gear mechanisms and cables. Make sure you have a pump, a bell, a rear rack to carry panniers and, if cycling at night, a set of working lights.

Preparing yourself

Equipping the family with cycling clothing need not be an expensive exercise. Comfort is the key when considering what to wear. Essential items for well-being on a bike are padded cycling shorts, warm stretch leggings (avoid tight-fitting and seamed trousers like jeans or baggy tracksuit trousers that may become caught in the chain), stiff-soled training shoes, and a wind and waterproof jacket. Fingerless gloves will add to your comfort.

A cycling helmet provides essential protection if you fall off your bike, so they are particularly recommended for young children learning to cycle.

Wrap your child up with several layers in colder weather. Make sure you and those with you are easily visible by car drivers and other road users, by wearing light-coloured or luminous clothing in daylight and reflective strips or sashes in failing light and when it is dark.

What to take with you

Invest in a pair of medium-sized panniers (rucksacks are unwieldy and can affect balance) to carry the necessary gear for you and your family for the day. Take extra clothes with you, the amount depending on the season, and always pack a light wind/waterproof jacket. Carry a basic tool kit (tyre levers, adjustable spanner, a small screwdriver, puncture repair kit, a set of Allen keys) and practical spares, such as an inner tube, a universal brake/gear cable, and a selection of nuts and bolts. Also, always take a pump and a strong lock.

Cycling, especially in hilly terrain and off-road, saps energy, so take enough food and drink for your outing. Always carry plenty of water, especially in hot and humid weather conditions. Consume high-energy snacks like cereal bars, cake or fruits, eating little and often to combat feeling weak and tired. Remember that children get thirsty (and hungry) much more quickly than adults so always have food and diluted juices available for them.

And finally, the most important advice of all–enjoy yourselves!

Around the Moors Valley Country Park

Exploring woodland and lakes, with extra loops to create your own route.

A miniature railway

The tracks may only be 7.25 inches (18.5cm) wide, but there's a real railway atmosphere to the miniature line at the Moors Valley Country Park. Its steam locomotives, carriages and goods vans thread their way around a landscaped loop beside the Moors Lake, and the 1-mile (1.6km) circuit is complete with a station and four tunnels.

The Moors Lake itself was built as a 'safety valve' to contain flooding in the area, which is liable after heavy rainfall. Some of the spoil from the lake was used to landscape the golf course and these developments provided the inspiration for the 1,500-acre (608ha) country park.

Work on the miniature railway began in 1985 as tracks were laid out and Kingsmere station was created from former farm buildings on the site. Many of the locomotives, rolling stock and carriages were brought from the Tucktonia Leisure Centre at Christchurch, and the new line opened to the public in July 1986. The railway is popular with both adults and children, and the ten-minute ride takes you past the main signal box and along the banks of the lake before looping around the play area on the way back to Kingsmere station. The railway is open daily from late May to early September, as well as during Easter and the Christmas holidays.

the ride

1 Leave the car park by the road entrance, zig-zag across **Hurn Lane** and join the combined cycleway/pavement under the A31. Bear left past the **phone-box**, then stop at the A31 slip road. Cross with care, then bear left on to the **Castleman Trail** towards Ashley Heath. The narrow gravel track bears to the right and pulls clear of the A31 through a tunnel of **young oak trees**. Soon the old line widens out into a 'dual carriageway' of narrow tracks separated by gorse and brambles. Watch out for cars as you cross the lane at **Holly**

A packed model railway ride through Moors Valley Country Park

Grove Farm. You'll speed along the next section to the road crossing at **Ashley Heath**. Stop here, and cross **Horton Road** with care. There's a convenience shop on your right as you rejoin the Castleman Trail and continue along the tree-shaded **cycleway**. Very soon, pass a section of the **former platform** at Ashley Heath, complete with its railway name-board. Continue for 600yds (549m), then look out for the narrow exit into **Forest Edge Drive** on the right.

2 Go through here and follow this residential road to the T-junction with Horton Road. Take care as you zig-zag left and right into the **Moors Valley Country Park** – it's only 50yds (46m), but you may prefer to wheel your bike along the pavement beside this busy road. Follow the tarred entrance road for the last 0.5 mile (800m) to reach the **visitor centre**, with a restaurant, toilets and other facilities. For the shortest ride, turn here and retrace the outward route back to the start. But it's well worth extending your visit by picking up a park map and following one of the four waymarked cycle routes around the forest.

3 The **Corsican Circuit** (2 miles/3.2km) is the basic ring at the heart of the park, which you can extend by adding one or more of the loops. It leads east from the visitor centre and loops anti-clockwise. The level route passes the **Play Trail entrance**, then circles back on good, gravelled forest rides.

4 Take the **Watchmoor Loop** (1.5 miles/ 2.3km) off the Corsican Circuit. It follows sandy tracks in the quieter areas of the forest. You'll see areas of open woodland where the smell of the pines mixes with the

2h00 | **12 MILES** | **19.3 KM** | **LEVEL 123**

SHORTER ALTERNATIVE ROUTE

1h00 | **5.5 MILES** | **8.8 KM** | **LEVEL 123**

MAP: OS Explorer OL22 New Forest
START/FINISH: Ashley Twinning (free) car park; grid ref: SU139048
TRAILS/TRACKS: old railway cycleway, roads and forest tracks
LANDSCAPE: the tree-lined old railway leads into mixed woodland, heath and lakes
PUBLIC TOILETS: Moors Valley Country Park
TOURIST INFORMATION: Ringwood, tel: 01425 470896
CYCLE HIRE: Moors Valley Country Park visitor centre, tel: 01425 470721
THE PUB: The Old Beams, Ibsley
⚠ Two main road crossings and slow-moving traffic on country park access road. Suitability: inexperienced riders and children over 7 depending on trail option selected

Getting to the start
The car park is 0.5 miles (800m) south west of Ringwood off the A31. Leave the A31 at the B3081 junction, then take the Hurn Lane exit from the junction roundabout for the car park.

Why do this cycle ride?
A versatile route: at its simplest, you'll follow a level, traffic-free cycleway to the Moors Valley Country Park, with its superb range of family-friendly facilities and attractions. You can extend or vary this basic route by following one or more of the traffic-free cycle trails within the park.

Researched and written by: David Foster

Moors Valley

HAMPSHIRE

sweet scent of bracken, before rejoining the Corsican Circuit.

5 At this point you can also detour off on the **Somerley Loop** (1 mile/1.6km). This weaves its way over gravel and dirt tracks through some of the denser parts of the forest, though there are still some wide heather verges in places. It is the most undulating of the park trails, with a steep downhill section near the end.

6 The Somerley Loop joins on to the **Crane Loop** (2 miles/3.2km), which on its own is great for young families. This pretty route heads out beside the **golf course** and **Crane Lake**, before returning beside the miniature railway. You'll mainly follow along smoothly tarred trails, though there are some gravel and dirt sections, too. Be alert and watch out for cars and other vehicles on the final section, which shares one of the park roads.

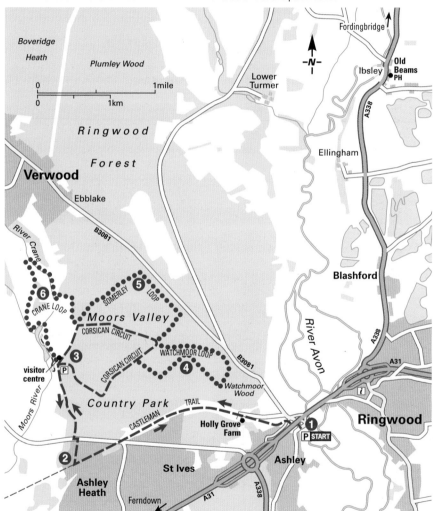

The Old Beams

The exterior of this 600-year-old cruck-beamed cottage is everything you would expect of an untouched country pub. The roof is neatly thatched, the walls are half-timbered and the building is flanked by an orchard garden. But all is not what it seems. Venturing inside is like entering Dr Who's Tardis, and beyond the pretty façade you will find a vast open-plan area, with a conservatory-style extension dominated by a central hooded fireplace. Furnishings range from dark wood tables and chairs to pine farmhouse tables. Along one side is the grand buffet table, laden with cold meats, seafood and fresh salads, drawing diners all day long.

about the pub

The Old Beams
Salisbury Road, Ibsley
Ringwood, Hampshire BH24 3PP
Tel: 01425 473387

DIRECTIONS: beside the A338 Ringwood-to-Salisbury road, 3 miles (4.8km) north of Ringwood
PARKING: 100
OPEN: daily, all day
FOOD: daily, all day
BREWERY/COMPANY: Greene King Brewery
REAL ALE: Greene King IPA & Abbot Ale, Ringwood Best

Food

In addition to the usual sandwiches and ploughman's, there's a buffet counter displaying a wide range of cold meats and salads. Hot dishes include steak and ale pie, fish and chips, lamb slow cooked with rosemary and red wine on thyme mash, mixed grill and chargrilled tuna with white wine and coriander sauce. Sunday roast carvery lunches are served all afternoon.

Family facilities

Expect a genuine welcome, with smaller portions and standard children's menu available. There are also high chairs and baby-changing facilities.

Alternative refreshment stops

Seasons Restaurant at Moors Valley Country Park serves breakfast, lunch and afternoon tea.

☛ Where to go from here

At the Dorset Heavy Horse Centre near Verwood you'll see magnificent Shire horses, meet and groom donkeys and miniature Shetland ponies, and help feed the many animals at the centre, including Lulu the llama. Café, picnic and play areas (www.dorset-heavy-horse-centre.co.uk).

A circuit around Linwood

Venture off the beaten track and mix with wildlife in the heart of the New Forest.

New Forest deer

You'll often see deer along this trail, especially early in the morning or around dusk – go quietly for the best chance of seeing these timid woodland residents in their natural habitat. Keep an eye out for roe deer in the cultivated fields close to Dockens Water, between the start of the ride and the point where you join the tarred lane leading up to the Red Shoot Inn. These graceful creatures are 24–28 inches

(61–71cm) high at the shoulder and the males have short, forked antlers. Roe deer have rich reddish-brown coats from May to September, but turn greyer in winter and develop a white patch on the rump.

You'll occasionally spot red deer in the same area, especially on the open heath near Black Barrow. These are our largest native species, and a fully-grown male with his splendid russet coat and impressive antlers may stand nearly 4ft (1.2m) tall at the shoulder. The males are at their boldest when competing for females during the mating season in early autumn.

Fallow deer may pop up almost anywhere on the ride, but a favourite haunt

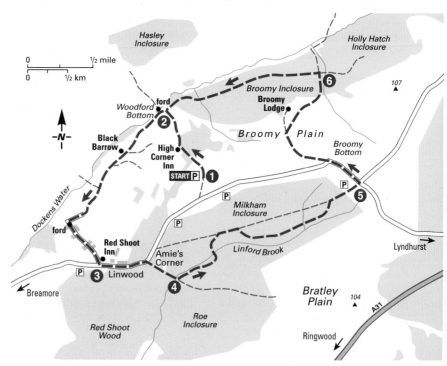

is in Broomy Bottom, off to your right as you cross Broomy Plain. With their reddish-fawn coats dappled with white spots, these appealing animals have white rumps and a black line running up the tail. The males have broad antlers and stand up to 3ft (0.9m) tall at the shoulder.

the ride

1 Turn right out of the car park and pass the end of the gravel track which leads up to the **High Corner Inn**.

2 At Woodford Bottom bear left at the wooden barrier on your right and pass the ford across the Dockens Water stream, also on your right. Keep to the waymarked cycle route as it follows the gravelled track that winds across the open heath, past a few scattered houses and the tree-capped mound of **Black Barrow**. A few smaller tracks lead off to left and right, but the main gravelled trail is easy enough to follow. Keep straight on as a similar track leads in from your left near the thatched Bogmyrtle Cottage, until you join a tarred lane. Almost at once the lane turns sharp left through a tiny ford and climbs gently up to the road junction at the **Red Shoot Inn**.

3 Turn left opposite the post-box, still following the waymarked cycle route, and continue to climb until the road levels off and swings to the left at **Amie's Corner**. Fork right here, sticking with the waymarked cycle route as it joins a gravelled forest track. The trail dives into Milkham Inclosure through wooden gates beside an attractive whitewashed cottage, then drops to a bridge over the Linford Brook.

1h45 · **7 MILES** · **11.3 KM** · **LEVEL 123**

MAP: OS Explorer OL22 New Forest
START/FINISH: Spring Bushes car park, Linwood; grid ref: SU196107
TRAILS/TRACKS: gravelled forest tracks, two short sections on rural lanes
LANDSCAPE: broadleaf and coniferous woodland interspersed with open heathland
PUBLIC TOILETS: none on route
TOURIST INFORMATION: Lyndhurst, tel: 023 8028 2269
CYCLE HIRE: Country Lanes, 9 Shaftesbury Street, Fordingbridge, tel: 01425 655022
THE PUB: The High Corner Inn, Linwood
❗ Moderate hills, some uneven and stony tracks. Suitable for older children, off-road riding experience useful

Getting to the start
Linwood is a village on a minor road north east of Ringwood. Spring Bushes car park is on the road that runs west from Emery Down, near Lyndhurst, to Rockford, just north of Ringwood.

Why do this cycle ride?
This relatively remote ride offers peace and quiet, and the opportunity to see the New Forest at its best. You'll follow waymarked Forestry Commission off-road cycle tracks deep into the heart of the Forest, with two short sections on tarred roads where you will need to watch out for the occasional car. There are plenty of opportunities for birdwatching or studying the other wildlife.

Researched and written by: David Foster

Linwood HAMPSHIRE

A family cycles through the countryside at Linwood

4 A few yards further on turn left at the numbered waymark post 5, then follow the track as it winds through open mixed woodland and re-crosses the **Linford Brook**. Continue as the track bears right at the next **waymark post**, then right again in front of a pair of wooden gates where you enter an area of mainly coniferous woodland. A pair of wooden gates punctuates your progress to the top of the hill, where further gates lead you out into the Forestry Commission's **Milkham car park**. Go through here, cross the car park, and stop at the road junction.

5 Turn left towards **Linwood** and follow the narrow tarred lane for 500yds (457m) until it bears away to the left. Fork right here on to the waymarked cycle trail that follows the gravel track towards **Broomy Lodge** and **Holly Hatch**. Here your route crosses the high heathland plateau of **Broomy Plain**. This is a

good spot to see birds such as Dartford warblers, meadow pipits and stonechats, and you'll also enjoy long views towards Cranborne Chase and the Wiltshire Downs. Bear right at the next fork and follow the trail down into **Holly Hatch Inclosure**.

6 At the foot of the hill, numbered **waymark post 3** stands at the forest crossroads. Turn left here, on to a lovely tree-shaded track with soft green verges that leads you through the **oak woods**. Two pairs of wooden gates mark your progress through the inclosure, and at length the oaks give way to conifers. Follow the waymarked trail until you rejoin your outward route at a low wooden barrier. Turn left here, and climb the short hill back to the **High Corner Inn**.

The High Corner Inn

The High Corner is an early 18th-century inn, much extended and modernised. It is set in 7 acres (2.8ha) of the New Forest and hidden down an old drovers' track off a narrow Forest lane. A quiet hideaway in winter, mobbed in high summer due to its heart-of-the-Forest location, it is a popular retreat for families, offering numerous bar-free rooms, an outdoor adventure playground and miles of easy New Forest walks. Although extensively refurbished, this rambling old building retains a wealth of beams, wooden and flagstone floors, and a blazing winter log fire in the cosy main bar. There's a separate food servery, plus top-notch Wadworth ales on tap and overnight accommodation in eight well-equipped rooms.

Food

An extensive printed menu includes sandwiches, ploughman's lunches and salads, as well as freshly battered haddock and chips, beef and 6X pie and sizzling steak platters. Look to the blackboard for daily soups, daily roasts or the likes of baked trout with pine nuts and chargrilled pork loin with spiced apple cream.

Family facilities

This is a great family pub – there's a children's menu, family areas, high chairs and a woodland garden equipped with its own adventure playground.

Alternative refreshment stops

Also owned by Wadworth Brewery, the Red Shoot Inn offers home-cooked meals and brews its own beer behind the pub.

about the pub

The High Corner Inn
Linwood, Ringwood
Hampshire BH24 3QY
Tel: 01425 473973

DIRECTIONS: a gravel track to the High Corner Inn branches off the road, 400yds (366m) west of the start point
PARKING: 200
OPEN: daily, all day in summer, and all day Sunday in winter
FOOD: daily, all day July and August
BREWERY/COMPANY: Wadworth Brewery
REAL ALE: Wadworth Henry's IPA, 6X and JCB
ROOMS: 7 en suite

☛ Where to go from here

Breamore House, north of here off the A338, is a handsome old manor house which dates back to 1583. It has a fine collection of paintings and china, and a countryside museum which includes steam engines (www.breamorehouse.com).

Linwood HAMPSHIRE

Through the Meon Valley from Soberton

Country lanes and an old railway trail lead you through the wooded Meon Valley.

The Meon Valley Railway

On your way through Brockbridge you'll pass the former Droxford Station, where a plaque beneath the post box records the railway's contribution to victory in World War II. Early in June 1944, Sir Winston Churchill and his War Cabinet met with other Allied leaders in a special train at Droxford Station to plan the D-Day invasion of Europe. The Meon Valley Railway's easy curves and wide bridges reflect its promoters' aspirations for a new main line to the south coast. Yet commercial realities dictated that the railway was opened with just a single line, and this quiet rural backwater was never upgraded to double track.

As well as the five stations between Alton and Fareham, goods sidings were opened at Farringdon and Mislingford, the latter handling traffic from the local timber trade that still continues to this day. As you enter Mislingford goods yard, look out for the remains of the Southern Railway loading gauge on your right – a curious concrete structure that resembles an old-fashioned gibbet. A curved metal bar once hung from this framework, at the correct height to check that loaded wagons emerging from the sidings would pass safely under bridges and tunnels on the line.

the ride

1 Outside The White Lion, turn left on to the village's main street, heading north towards **Brockbridge**. Go over the crest of the gentle hill, then enjoy the easy 1-mile (1.6km) ride down to the former **Droxford railway station** on your left, just before the junction with the B2150.

2 Turn left here under the old railway bridge, then immediately right into **Brockbridge Road**. After a short climb you can settle down for the pleasant ride into **Meonstoke**. Continue up the gently rising village street, then fork right towards **Pound Lane** and Stocks Farm. Almost at once bear left into **Rectory Lane**, and follow it through to the T-junction opposite Stocks Meadow.

3 Turn right and climb the short hill. After 400yds (366m) bear right under the **broken railway bridge**, then right again up the slope on to the old railway line. Bear left at the top on to the broad Meon Valley

The parish church and water meadows at Meonstoke

Trail, which follows the old line south through a tunnel of trees towards Droxford. Pass under two brick arches before approaching the former **Droxford Station** on a girder bridge over the B2150.

4 Follow as the trail swings right and skirts around the **station buildings** – now converted into a private house – before rejoining the old line and continuing as before. After 400yds (364m) an elegant **brick arch** carries a footpath overhead. A further 0.75 mile (1.2km) brings you to **Cut Bridge**.

5 For a shorter ride, you can climb up to the road here and cycle back past the church to **The White Lion** at Soberton. For the full route, continue under Cut Bridge and on for a further 2 miles (3.2km) to reach the former goods yard at **Mislingford**. There are some attractive gardens behind **Bridge Cottage** on your left, just before you pass under the brick arch bridge and

2h00 — **9.75 MILES** — **15.7 KM** — **LEVEL 123**

MAP: OS Explorer 119 Meon Valley
START/FINISH: by the White Lion, Soberton; grid ref: SU610168
TRAILS/TRACKS: wide off-road cycle trail (may be muddy after rain) with optional return on quiet country lanes
LANDSCAPE: rolling farmland and wooded hillsides frame the little river valley
PUBLIC TOILETS: Forestry Commission picnic site, Upperford Copse
TOURIST INFORMATION: Petersfield, tel: 01730 268829
CYCLE HIRE: Owens Cycles, Petersfield, tel: 01730 260446
THE PUB: The White Lion, Soberton

❗ Three short, steep hills, and traffic on the lanes and at the B2150 crossing in Droxford. Cycle trail may be muddy after rain. Suitable for older children with stamina and good traffic sense

Getting to the start

The hamlet of Soberton lies south east of Droxford, on a minor road off the A32. Park considerately in the village.

Why do this cycle ride?

This varied ride loops north through the villages of Brockbridge and Meonstoke before turning south along the cycle track that follows the former Meon Valley railway line. The trail leaves the old railway at the former Mislingford goods yard, and returns to Soberton along quiet country lanes. You can easily cut the route short if you wish, and there's also an optional diversion to the woodland picnic area at Upperford Copse.

Researched and written by: David Foster

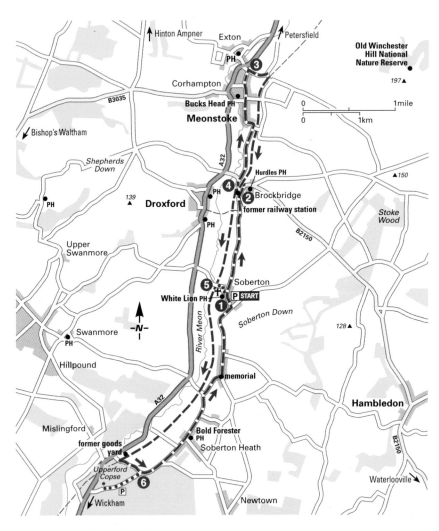

into Upperford Copse. Turn hard left immediately under the bridge, make your way up the **rough woodland track** to the road, and continue to the junction at the top of the hill.

6 A right turn here towards **Wickham** gives a short diversion to the Forestry Commission's **woodland picnic area** and toilets at Upperford Copse, about 0.33 mile (0.5km) down the road. To continue the main ride, turn left towards Soberton and follow the road past the **Bold Forester** to the bottom of **Horns Hill**. Bear right and climb the other side of the little valley to the junction at **Soberton's war memorial**. At this point turn left towards Soberton, drift down the long hill to the crossroads at Soberton Down, then turn left into **School Hill** towards Soberton and Droxford for the final 300yds (274m) back to The White Lion and the village green.

The White Lion

The White Lion is a traditional country pub situated near the church and opposite the village green, smack on the Wayfarer's Walk long-distance path. A 17th-century building, it has a cream-painted façade brightened by flower tubs and hanging baskets. A covered patio and secluded rear garden provide peaceful summer alfresco seating. The wood-floored main bar is rustic in style, with a wood-burning stove, simple wall benches, traditional pub games and a friendly atmosphere, while the carpeted lounge and dining areas are decorated with a range of prints and warmed by an open log fire.

Food

Expect traditional pub meals at lunchtime, such as the 'ultimate' ploughman's lunch and the 'Lion' sausage sandwich. Samples from the evening bill of fare might include sea bass with ginger and garlic, spicy lamb and chickpea casserole and and vegetarian options such as spinach cheesecake. The

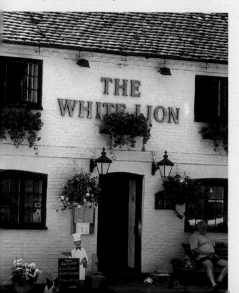

about the pub

The White Lion
School Hill, Soberton
Hampshire SO32 3PF
Tel: 01489 877346
www.thewhitelionsoberton.co uk

DIRECTIONS: see Getting to the start
PARKING: roadside parking
OPEN: daily, all day
FOOD: daily
BREWERY/COMPANY: free house
REAL ALE: Bass, Palmers 200, White Lion Bitter, guest beer

menu changes daily, so desserts such as whisky bread and butter pudding may be available. Food is made on the premises.

Family facilities
Children are welcome in the eating areas. High chairs are available.

Alternative refreshment stops
Pubs along the way include the The Hurdles at Droxford and the Bucks Head in Meonstoke.

☛ Where to go from here
To the north of here, just off the A272, Hinton Ampner is a restored Regency mansion with superb gardens which combine formal design with delightfully informal planting (www.nationaltrust.org.uk).

A circuit of Queen Elizabeth Country Park

A wooded ride through the heart of Hampshire's largest country park.

Butser Ancient Farm

Butser Ancient Farm was founded by Dr Peter Reynolds in 1972 to improve the understanding of prehistoric farming methods. The original farm was established west of the A3 at Rakefield Hanger, some 3 miles (4.8km) north of the present site. Although research continued at this remote location until 1989, Rakefield Hanger wasn't the ideal place to develop the farm's educational role. So, in 1976, a new site was developed at Hillhampton Down, just across the A3 from the country park visitor centre. This site boasted a large, thatched roundhouse, with fields of crops and an industrial research area for producing charcoal and early metals like iron, copper, tin and bronze. In 1991 the farm moved to its present site at Bascomb Copse, where the buildings, animals and crops recreate the living conditions on a British Iron Age farm about 2,300 years ago. The farm has a reception area with a video introduction, souvenir shop and toilets. There's also an activity centre where visitors can try their hand at grinding corn, spinning, weaving or making clay pots. The ancient farm is open to the public between March and September for weekend events, including

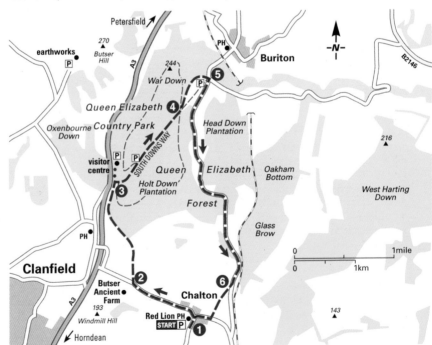

1h00 — **6 MILES** — **9.7 KM** — **LEVEL 123**

MAP: OS Explorer 120 Chichester

START/FINISH: public car park next to the Red Lion, Chalton; grid ref: SU731160

TRAILS/TRACKS: rough off-road trails, quiet rural lanes

LANDSCAPE: thickly wooded rolling chalk hills, with open fields grazed by sheep

PUBLIC TOILETS: Queen Elizabeth Country Park visitor centre

TOURIST INFORMATION: Petersfield, tel: 01730 268829

CYCLE HIRE: Owens Cycles, Petersfield, tel: 01730 260446

THE PUB: The Red Lion, Chalton

❗ There are two short, steep sections in the Country Park where you may prefer to push your bike; bumpy off-road tracks. Suitable for older children, some off-road experience useful

Cycling through Queen Elizabeth Country Park

demonstrations of prehistoric cookery, textiles and clothing.

the ride

1 Leave the car park and turn left past **The Red Lion,** then left again at the junction towards **Clanfield and Petersfield.** Pass under the power lines and continue for 700yds (640m) to the bottom of the hill opposite **Butser Ancient Farm.**

2 Fork right here on to the bridleway and **off-road cycle trail,** a bumpy track with lovely views across the fields to **Windmill Hill** and the ancient farm behind you on your left. The bridleway climbs steeply as it approaches the woods at the corner of the country park, and it's probably safer to dismount and push your bike at this point. Follow the bridleway as it skirts the western edge of the forest and drops gently down to the tarred **Forest Drive** and **picnic areas.**

3 Here you can turn left for the 300yds (274m) diversion to the park's **visitor centre,** with café and toilets. Alternatively, turn right to continue your ride. This

Getting to the start

Chalton lies east of the A3 between Petersfield and Horndean. Leave the A3 at the Clanfield exit, and follow signs to Chalton and the Red Lion pub (about 1 mile/1.6km). Bear right in the village and you'll find the public car park tucked away on the right hand side, just past the Red Lion.

Why do this cycle ride?

This route links Hampshire's oldest pub with its largest country park. Twenty miles of trails thread their way through the park's 1,400 acres (567ha) and you're sure to meet plenty of like-minded people enjoying themselves in the great outdoors. There's an excellent visitor centre, too, complete with shop, information desk and café. The route takes in a section of the South Downs Way national trail before returning to Chalton on a quiet country lane.

Researched and written by: David Foster

25

section, which follows part of the **South Downs Way** national trail, takes you past the **Benhams Bushes barbecue site** (advance booking required). Follow the Forest Drive for 600yds (549m). When you reach the hairpin bend, fork right through **Benhams Bushes car park** on to the waymarked off-road cycle trail. Follow the bumpy gravel road for just over 0.5 mile (800m) to a junction near the top of the hill.

4 Bear left here, then fork right a few yards further on, sticking with the gravel road as it drops to a **wooden gate** at the Forestry Commission's **Hall's Hill car park**. Continue through the car park and stop at the road exit.

5 Leave the South Downs Way here, and turn right on to the **narrow lane** that drops down towards Chalton and Finchdean. This easy ride takes you through a deeply rural, **wooded landscape**; sheep graze in small open fields between the beechwoods and hazel coppices, and you may spot the occasional deer. Eventually you'll pass under a line of **electricity wires**, before the road climbs around a right-hand bend and runs beside the railway for a short distance. Two hundred yards (183m) further on, look out for a **signposted byway** on your right-hand side.

6 Fork right here for the short, sharp climb up on to **Chalton Peak**. There are fine views on your right towards Windmill Hill, with dog rose, bramble and knapweed colouring the hedges beside this pleasant, level section. At the end of the byway turn right for the final 200yds (183m) back to the junction where you fork left to return to The Red Lion and the car park.

Negotiating a bend on a woodland path in the Queen Elizabeth Country Park

The Red Lion

feel-good puddings such as cherry pie and delicious bread and butter pudding.

Family facilities
Children are welcome in the dining room (where there's a small standard children's menu) and the spacious rear garden. The latter offers lovely views to Windmill Hill and Butser Ancient Farm.

Alternative refreshment stops
The Coach House Café in Queen Elizabeth Country Park or the Five Bells in Buriton.

☛ Where to go from here
Gale's Brewery at Horndean has tours and a shop (www.galesales.co.uk).

This beautiful timbered and thatched pub – a typical Hampshire cottage, reputedly built in the 12th century as dwellings for the craftsmen building the parish church – stands at the heart of the quaint village, opposite the lych-gate. Tourists, walkers and weary A3 travellers are attracted into its cosy and rustic main bar and modern dining bar extension – not least for the tip-top ale and the impressive range of whiskies and country wines. Both the old-fashioned public bar and the lounge bar are contained in the original building, the high-backed old settles of the former providing the perfect foil to the black beams and huge inglenook. This is reputedly Hampshire's oldest pub, and it has recently changed hands, now being run by Fullers Brewery.

Food
In addition to the sandwiches and filled baguettes (hot roasted vegetables), the ploughman's lunches and filled jacket potatoes, daily specials may include home-made steak and ale pie, traditional roast beef, specialist sausages, and old-fashioned

about the pub

The Red Lion
Chalton, Waterlooville
Hampshire PO8 0BG
023 9259 2246
www.gales.co.uk

DIRECTIONS: in the centre of the village
PARKING: use adjacent village car park
OPEN: daily; all day
FOOD: daily
BREWERY/COMPANY: Fullers Brewery
REAL ALE: London Pride, Discovery, HSB and seasonal ales

Chalton HAMPSHIRE

The Centurion Way from Chichester

Encounter the sculptures along the Centurion Way cycle route, and scale the Iron Age banks of The Trundle.

The Centurion Way and The Trundle
This traffic-free bike and pedestrian trail opened in full in 2002, and was named the Centurion Way because it crosses a Roman road at one point. For most of its length it follows the trackbed of a defunct railway that ran between Chichester and Midhurst. This existed from 1881 until 1957; the stretch southwards from Lavant was kept in operation for transporting sugar beet and gravel up to 1991. Along this route you will see some highly quirky modern sculptures: two of these, Roman Archway and Primary Hangers, were made with the enthusiastic help of local schoolchildren.

Huge grassy banks on The Trundle mark the extent of an Iron Age hill fort, which has two modern masts on it. The view is quite spectacular, including almost the entire east coast of the Isle of Wight, the watery expanses of Chichester Harbour and the stands of Goodwood racecourse. If you look carefully on a clear day, you can see the chalk cliffs of the Seven Sisters way over to the east, and the white tent-like structure of

Butlin's in Bognor Regis. There is no access for cyclists to the top, so lock up your bike by the car park and walk up.

the ride

1 Take the **Centurion Way** (signposted as cycle path to Lavant) to the right of the house at the end of the road, and to the left of the **school gates**. This joins the old railway track by a sculpture called **Roman Archway**, which spans the track. After going under a bridge, you will see the entrance to **Brandy Hole Copse**, a local nature reserve to the left. Among the oak coppice and chestnut trees are high, overgrown banks that were erected 2,000 years ago by a late Iron Age tribe as boundaries or fortifications, some years before the Roman Conquest in AD 43. Dragonflies and bats are attracted to this reserve, which also has three ponds to explore.

2 Before going under the next bridge (signposted Lavant), you will see sculptures called **The Chichester Road Gang**, resembling road workers carrying tools, but made out of metal canisters. Away to the left is another artwork called the **Roman Amphitheatre**. It is here that the now invisible Roman road once passed.

3 After the next bridge, with its **dangling metal sculptures** – Primary Hangers – the route leaves the old railway track and joins a residential road in Mid Lavant. Just down to the right is an excellent **adventure playground**. Carry along the road, following

Roman Amphitheatre is one of several unusual works of art on the route

Cycling along a quiet lane on the route

3h00	11 MILES	17.7 KM	LEVEL 1 2 **3**

SHORTER ALTERNATIVE ROUTE

1h30	10.5 MILES	16.9 KM	LEVEL **1** 2 3

MAP: OS Explorer 120 Chichester

START/FINISH: Westgate, Chichester, at the end of the road by the railway line and Bishop Luffa School; grid ref: SU847047

TRAILS/TRACKS: surfaced cycle path, compacted earth cycle path; full ride returns via chalk field track, stony track and roads

LANDSCAPE: old railway track, woodland, farmland; chalk downland on the full ride

PUBLIC TOILETS: none on route

TOURIST INFORMATION: Chichester, tel: 01243 775888

CYCLE HIRE: Shed End Bikes, Preston Farm, near West Dean (on this route) tel: 01243 811766, 07946 341685

THE PUB: The Selsey Arms, West Dean

❶ The full ride has long, stony descent: ride with care and wheel your bike if necessary. There's a short section along the main road

Getting to the start

Turn off the A27 on the western side of Chichester, along the A259 into Chichester. Turn left at the roundabout, then left at the next mini-roundabout, along Westgate. Roadside parking at the end of the road.

Why do this cycle ride?

There is some weird and wonderful sculpture as well as an adventure playground along the Centurion Way, a level path shared with walkers. From the fringes of Chichester, head out into the country, reaching West Dean. Either return the same way, or take a more demanding off-road route up to The Trundle.

Researched and written by: Tim Locke

signs for West Dean. After concrete bollards, and soon after a **postbox** on the left, then St Mary's Close on the right, turn right at a **square green** to rejoin the old railway track (not signposted at time of writing). Later the Centurion Way turns left to leave the old railway track, then turns right along a cycle path parallel to the **A286**.

4 This path ends at the village of **West Dean**. Turn right along the small road, round the back of the village (take the next turning on the left for **The Selsey Arms**, or to see the churchyard, with its fine old tombstones, carry straight on). For the short route, return the same way to the start. For the full route bear to the right where the road first bends left, towards ornate **iron gates** in a flint wall. Follow the bridleway uphill, alongside the wall and along the field edge, and later through a forest. Finally emerge at the top as the view opens out by a **house**. Keep forward on a track to a car park.

5 Before turning right (towards the sea) to continue, walk up ahead to the summit of **The Trundle**, marked by two prominent **masts**, to enjoy the view. Now carefully ride the stony route down a long hill to **East Lavant**. Turn right along the main village street, avoiding a left fork, and past the Royal Oak. Ignore side turns and go past a **triangular recreation ground** on your right.

6 Turn left along the **A286** for 350yds (320m). Take the first turning on the right (with the cycle route sign for Chichester) by stopping at a small lay-by (just before this turning) on the left and then crossing the road when it is safe to do so. After crossing the bridge, turn left to rejoin the **Centurion Way**, and turn right to return to the start.

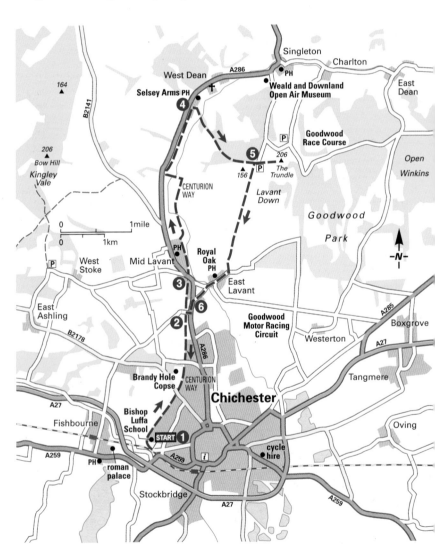

The Selsey Arms

The Selsey Arms is a traditional late 18th-century village pub, well placed for Goodwood, the Weald and Downland Museum and visitors heading to West Dean Gardens. The front bar rooms feature bare boards, horse brasses on beams, dark wood pub tables and chairs, and a friendly, welcoming atmosphere. Daily papers are strewn on a table for customers to read. There's a separate, carpeted restaurant with open fires, beamed ceilings and plain wooden furnishings.

Food

Good-value bar food ranges from sandwiches and ham ploughman's to haddock and chips and home-made steak and kidney pie. A blackboard highlights the bargain two-course lunch and evening extras, such as lamb's liver and bacon, red bream, and smoked haddock topped with Welsh rarebit.

Family facilities

Children are welcome inside the pub. The sheltered patio with picnic benches is ideal in fine weather.

Alternative refreshment stops

Try the Royal Oak, East Lavant (on full ride only) or the café at the Weald and Downland Open Air Museum (if visiting).

☛ Where to go from here

The Weald and Downland Open Air Museum (www.wealddown.co.uk) at Singleton, 1 mile (1.6km) east of West Dean, can be reached by driving or cycling along the A286. More than 45 historic buildings, from medieval to Victorian, rescued from south east England, have been rebuilt here. About 0.75 mile (1.2km) along a signposted route from the beginning of this ride or by car via the A259, is Fishbourne Roman Palace (www.sussexpast.co.uk). The largest Roman building north of the Alps, it has outstanding mosaics.

about the pub

The Selsey Arms
West Dean, Chichester
West Sussex PO18 0QX
Tel: 01243 811465

DIRECTIONS: on the A286 at West Dean, between Singleton and Mid Lavant
PARKING: 20
OPEN: daily
FOOD: daily
BREWERY/COMPANY: free house
REAL ALE: Ringwood, Ruddles and changing guest ales

Amberley and Bignor Roman Villa

A tour of sandy forests and heathland, and thatched villages snuggling below the South Downs.

Amberley and Bignor

The little knot of streets in Amberley is worth exploring house by house: an extraordinary number of them are thatched or half-timbered. At the start or finish of the ride, follow the no-through road past the church to reach the outer wall of the medieval castle. It is now a hotel and not open to the public, but is worth a look for its marvellous position, brooding over the marshy meadow known as Amberley Wild Brooks, a rich haunt of birdlife, including teal and Bewick swans.

As you approach Bignor Roman Villa, all you see is a series of strange thatched huts. These shelter what is one of the finest Roman villas ever discovered in Britain. It was found in 1811 by farmer Joseph Tupper who was ploughing the land here when he unearthed a magnificent mosaic floor depicting Ganymede's abduction by an eagle. It was soon realised how important this mostly 4th century AD building was, and the farmer quickly made it into a tourist attraction, erecting these shelters. Many Roman villas were deliberately built in locations with extremely beautiful views, and Bignor is no exception.

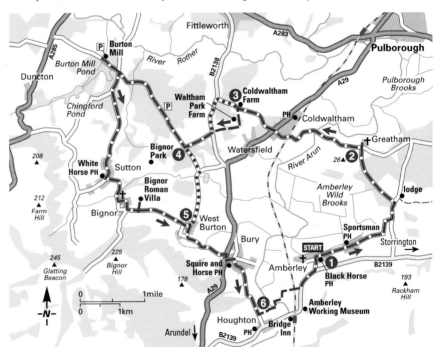

the ride

1 With The Black Horse on your right and the White House on your left follow the road out of Amberley. Past the **Sportsman pub**, turn left at a T-junction (signposted Greatham). By a building on the left you will see some **sandstone crags** away to the left, an inviting feature for children to clamber up. Turn left at the next junction, signposted Greatham. (If you carry on a short way towards Wiggonholt you will reach the lodge on the right at the edge of Parham Park; from here a ten-minute walk into the estate gives you a good distant view of the grand Elizabethan house.)

2 At the next junction, turn left to **Coldwaltham**, but first detour ahead along a track to **Greatham church** (soon reached via a gate on the right). This is a lovely, unspoilt church with no electricity – it's lit by oil lamps – and with ancient beam structures known as kingposts supporting the roof. The route soon crosses **Greatham Bridge**, with its ten rather wonky arches (a footpath on the near side gives access to the river bank and a lovely view). Wheel across the A29 carefully and take the road ahead signposted **Fittleworth**.

3 After **Coldwaltham Farm** on the right, turn left on a farm road towards **Waltham Park Farm** (if you prefer to avoid the off-road section, do not turn off here; instead carry on to the B2138, turn left then take the first right, signposted Bignor). Fork left at the farm, down an eroded **rocky track**, and turn right at the bottom on a **signposted bridleway** (avoiding the

---

3h00 — **15 MILES** — **24.1 KM** — **LEVEL 123**

SHORTER ALTERNATIVE ROUTE

2h15 — **11 MILES** — **17.7 KM** — **LEVEL 123**

MAP: OS Explorer 121 Arundel and Pulborough

START/FINISH: The Black Horse, Amberley village centre; grid ref: TQ030132

TRAILS/TRACKS: nearly all on quiet roads, with a short section over fields and along well-drained but very sandy tracks; a road alternative is provided

LANDSCAPE: woodland, wetland, parkland, farmland and views of the South Downs

PUBLIC TOILETS: none on route

TOURIST INFORMATION: Arundel, tel: 01903 882268

CYCLE HIRE: City Cycles, 44 Bognor Road, Chichester, West Sussex, tel: 01243 539992

THE PUB: The Black Horse, Amberley

🛈 Dismount to cross the A29. The off-road section at Point 3 avoids the B2138, which can be busy, but you will have to push your bike along a soft, sandy path. The full ride has two steep hills

Getting to the start

Turn off the B2139 between Storrington and the A29 at a sign for Amberley and the Black Horse. Park on roadside.

Why do this cycle ride?

From the thatched village of Amberley, the route heads along quiet lanes looking up to the South Downs, before passing silent country estates, timber-framed cottages and the entrance to Bignor Roman Villa. You might spot birds over the wetland of Amberley Wild Brooks.

Researched and written by: Tim Locke

signposted footpath just before). The route is sandy and you will have to push most of the way. Cross the B2138, taking the road ahead signposted Bignor.

Previous page: Detail from a mosaic found at the Roman Villa at Bignor
Above: A large cottage in Amberley

4 For the short route turn left in front of the gates to **Bignor Park** to follow signs for **Bignor Roman Villa**; keep right at the first junction and rejoin the main route in West Burton. For the full route, turn right at the gates. Pass a large heath – **Lord's Piece** – grazed by ponies on the left; this is the last site in Britain where you can find field crickets. At the top, keep left towards **Duncton**. At the next junction go straight ahead to **Burton Pond**, which was created for the long-vanished iron industry and which once powered Burton Mill (occasionally open in summer). Here you may spot kingfishers, bitterns and great crested grebes, and there's a nature trail that skirts the pond. Return to the junction and turn right towards **Sutton**. Turn left in Sutton, by the **White Horse pub**, following signs to Bignor, and pass a wonderful

thatched, half-timbered 15th-century house called Yeoman's House. After Bignor church continue to Bignor Roman Villa, then carry on to West Burton.

5 In West Burton take the road signposted to Bury, crossing the **A29** by the traffic island and taking the road opposite and to the right to **Bury**. Turn right in the village, towards **Houghton**.

6 After 1 mile (1.6km) turn left on the **South Downs Way** (marked with blue arrows) and follow the waymarkers across two fields, turning right on the river bank, over the **river bridge** and right on the other side, then left. At the **B2139**, turn left and take the first road on the left back into **Amberley**.

The Black Horse

The Black Horse is a lovely old pub at the heart of this beautiful South Downs village, often called the 'Pearl of Sussex'. One of several knocked-through cottages, it has been nicely revamped, with flagstones, dark red walls, log fires, old pictures and prints on the walls, and heavy beams hung with sheep bells and shepherd's tools, donated by the last shepherd to have a flock on the South Downs.

Food

Good traditional bar food is served throughout the pub. Choices include sandwiches (with salad and chips), ploughman's lunches, lasagne, steak and ale pie and home-made curries. Evening dishes may include rack of lamb and fillet steak with tiger prawns.

Family facilities

Children over the age of six are allowed in the bar and restaurant if they are well behaved and eating with their parents. On fine days head for the lovely walled garden.

Alternative refreshment stops

Try the Sportsman, just east of Amberley, the White Horse in Sutton or the Squire and Horse on the A29 at Bury. Burton Mill sometimes serves teas in high summer (tel: 01798 869575 to check first). There is also Houghton Bridge Riverside Tea Garden and Restaurant and The Bridge Inn just off the route near Amberley Working Museum and by the B2139 river bridge.

☛ Where to go from here

Set in a disused chalk pit Amberley Working Museum (www.amberleymuseum.co.uk) is an open-air museum giving an absorbing look at the industrial heritage of the south east, and featuring transport, electricity, telecommunications, industries such as printing, a wheelwright's and resident craftspeople – among them a blacksmith and a clay-pipe maker. Visit the Roman Villa at Bignor along the route (www.romansinsussex.co.uk).

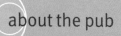

about the pub

The Black Horse
High Street, Amberley
West Sussex BN18 9LR
Tel: 01798 831552

DIRECTIONS: at the north end of the village: from the B2139, drive into Amberley keeping right at the junction; the pub is on the next corner

PARKING: street parking only

OPEN: daily; all day

FOOD: daily; all day Sunday

BREWERY/COMPANY: Punch Taverns

REAL ALE: Greene King IPA, Charles Wells Bombardier

Amberley WEST SUSSEX

Ditchling Beacon and the Chattri War Memorial

One of the most spectacular sections of the South Downs, with views all the way.

Jack and Jill windmills

A hundred years ago the South Downs were dotted with windmills. These two are among the last to survive. Jill Windmill (www.jillwindmill.org.uk) is a wooden corn mill, restored to working order and open free of charge in the afternoon on most summer Sundays and bank holidays. Built in Brighton in 1821, it was originally called Lashmar's Mill. Neighbouring Jack Windmill is a brick tower mill, built in 1866 and now a private house, but you can see it from the car park. They both fell into disuse around 1906 and were probably first nicknamed Jack and Jill in the 1920s.

Chattri War Memorial

The white, Sicilian marble war memorial, inscribed in English and Hindi, is a strangely exotic feature in the Sussex countryside. Erected in 1921, it is dedicated to Indian servicemen who lost their lives in World War I. Some 4,000 were taken to a temporary hospital in Brighton's Royal Pavilion (which must have seemed a very strange place to find themselves in). The Hindus and Sikhs who did not survive were cremated here in funeral pyres sprinkled with symbolic offerings such as fruits, flowers and spices in accordance with their religious customs.

the ride

1 Turn left out of the car park, signposted **'public bridleway to Ditchling Beacon'**

and immediately ignore a private driveway on the left to Jack Windmill and another track to the left. Soon fork left uphill at a junction, signposted **South Downs Way** (the right turn goes to a farm). Blue arrow markers with acorn motifs denote the South Downs Way, which you follow for most of the ride. The track rises quite steeply at first and is stony, but it soon levels out and becomes less rough. There are huge views northwards over the Weald and you can see the Surrey hills in the distance. The escarpment is too steep for ploughing, and the wildlife is relatively undisturbed. Nine types of orchid, including the bee orchid (named for obvious reasons) grow hereabouts, and you may spot a pale blue chalkhill butterfly.

2 From **Ditchling Beacon car park** cross the road carefully and take the **South Downs Way** opposite. You will pass one of two dew ponds on the route: this is a man-made feature, created for livestock to drink from, and has a clay lining to stop water draining into the porous chalk. The route climbs up two grassy rises and drops slightly to cross a narrow farm road. From here it becomes clay rather than chalk on the surface, and can be sticky after rain.

3 After the next left, a descending fork (which you avoid), look for a **track** on the right, marked with a blue arrow which leads to a group of trees at the end of the field. This is the site of **Plumpton Plain**, a Bronze Age settlement. Carry on along the South Downs Way.

4 Just beyond a gate is a National Trust sign for **Black Cap**. Walk up to the summit by forking left to the **trig point**.

Chattri War Memorial

3h00 — **11 MILES** — **17.7 KM** — **LEVEL 123**

MAP: OS Explorer 122 South Downs Way:
Steyning to Newhaven

START/FINISH: free car park by Jack and Jill
windmills; grid ref: TQ304134. Alternative
start: Ditchling Beacon car park, south of
Ditchling; grid ref: TQ333131

TRAILS/TRACKS: quite bumpy chalk and
grass tracks, with some sections along clay

LANDSCAPE: chalk downland

PUBLIC TOILETS: none on route

TOURIST INFORMATION: Brighton,
tel: 0906 711 2255

CYCLE HIRE: Lifecycle, The Tile House,
Preston Park, Preston Road, Brighton tel:
01273 542425 (www.lifecyclebrighton.com)

THE PUB: The Bull, Ditchling

🚫 An energetic ride, with several ascents
and descents – not suitable for young children

Getting to the start

Jack and Jill windmills: follow the A273
south from Hassocks, past junctions on the
left with the B2112 and turning to Clayton,
then turn left just before Pyecombe up Mill
Lane. Ditchling Beacon: follow the B2112
south, then fork left on the road leading up
to Ditchling Beacon. The car park is on the
right at the very top (begin at Point 2).

Why do this cycle ride?

This is a challenging ride, but don't be too
put off by the beginning. After that there are
some lovely sections on the grassy Downs on
either side of Ditchling Beacon. You can
either ride from Jack and Jill to Ditchling
Beacon and back, continue to Black Cap, or
go along tracks to the Chattri Indian war
memorial and back to Jack and Jill.

Researched and written by: Tim Locke

Enjoy the view which stretches to Seaford
Head, a prominent, square-looking sea
cliff, and to the Downs near Lewes. Return
the same way, to **Ditchling Beacon**.

5 Unless you want to return along the
South Downs Way, turn left at the very
top of the main ascent after Ditchling
Beacon (where **Jack Windmill** comes into
view ahead). It's marked with a blue arrow
and a sign for **'Chattri and the windmills'**
(just after another junction by a signpost on
the right marked as the 'Keymer Post', while
left is signposted to Brighton). Carry on
down, with Brighton in view ahead, and at
the second gate (with a waymarker symbol
marked 'Chattri and the windmills' and with
the number 13 on it), detour ahead to see
the **Chattri War Memorial**.

6 After the next gate, you'll see the
memorial just down on your left. Leave
your bike at the top and walk down. Return
to the junction at the previous gate and turn
left, following signs: the route bends right
(number 44) on a fenced path slightly
uphill, left (number 45), then downhill and
turns right leaving the indicated route to
'Chattri and the windmills' (at number 46),
which continues ahead. The track drops
and rises, crossing the South Downs Way.
passing through a farm to reach Jack and
Jill windmills.

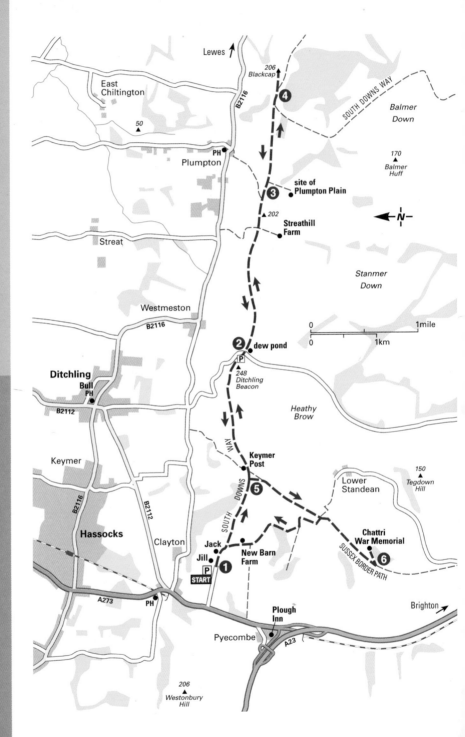

Lewes ↑

East
Chiltington

B2116

206
▲ Blackcap

❹

SOUTH DOWNS WAY

Balmer
Down

50
▲

PH
Plumpton

❸   site of
Plumpton Plain

170
▲
Balmer
Huff

202 ▲

Streathill
Farm

Streat

—N—

Stanmer
Down

Westmeston

B2116

❷   dew pond

P

248
Ditchling
Beacon

0   1mile
0   1km

Ditchling
Bull
PH

B2112

Heathy
Brow

Keymer

B2116

Keymer
Post

❺

Lower
Standean

150
▲
Tegdown
Hill

B2112

SOUTH   DOWNS   WAY

Hassocks

Clayton

Jack
Jill
P
START

❶

New Barn
Farm

Chattri
War Memorial

❻

SUSSEX BORDER PATH

A273

PH

Plough
Inn

Brighton →

Pyecombe

A23

206
▲
Westonbury
Hill

The Bull

Standing in a picturesque street in Ditchling, at the base of the South Downs, The Bull is a welcoming 14th-century beamed inn that has been comfortably refurbished. In the Inglenook Bar is an enormous fireplace with a roaring log fire in winter, low ceilings, old settles and dark wooden furnishings that give the room an ancient, time-worn feeling. Step into the Poacher's Bar and the décor is more modern, with large dining tables, Shaker-style chairs, an open fire and modern art lining the walls. Expect home-cooked food and four handpumped real ales.

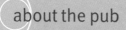

about the pub

The Bull
2 High Street, Ditchling
Brighton, East Sussex BN6 8TZ
Tel: 01273 843147

DIRECTIONS: drive down to the A273, turn right towards Hassocks, then first right to Ditchling; The Bull is in the centre of the village by the crossroads (park in the pub car park or the free public car park opposite). From Ditchling Beacon, turn left out of the car park and follow the road down to Ditchling

PARKING: 25

OPEN: daily; all day

FOOD: daily

BREWERY/COMPANY: free house

REAL ALE: Harveys Best, Timothy Taylor's, guest beers

ROOMS: 4 en suite

Food

The interesting menu includes sandwiches, dishes of marinated olives, home-made soups and main meals such as medallions of pork fillet with roasted vegetables, sausages and mash, marinated Halloumi, and feta and vegetable brochette.

Family facilities

Children are welcome throughout the pub and smaller portions of adult dishes are available. Lovely sun-trap side terrace with views of the village and South Downs.

Alternative refreshment stops

There may be an ice-cream van in the car park at Ditchling Beacon.

☛ Where to go from here

Brighton (www.visitbrighton.com) is in view for much of this ride. It lies some 5 miles (8km) south and is an easy drive via the A23. In warmer months there's a lot happening along the waterfront, including beach volleyball, craft and books stalls and fortune tellers. The Royal Pavilion is a fantastically lavish seaside palace built by George IV, an Indian fantasy that becomes rather more Chinese inside. Just across the little park, there's the free Brighton Museum and Art Gallery which has something for everyone.

Hamsey and Barcombe Mills

Peaceful hamlets, mill pools, Roman sites, a pub that offers boat hire and a fair-weather extension to see a steam railway.

The Lavender Line

Old advertising signs and railway paraphernalia adorn the beautifully painted and restored station at Isfield. If you visit Cinders Buffet, on the platform, you can see 'before and after' photos that show how much volunteers and lovers of this little country railway have put into running a short section of the line that once ran from Lewes to Uckfield. Steam and diesel trains run during most weekends throughout the year, and on some other days during summer; one ticket allows you to ride all day. You can also go into the signal box at Isfield, try pulling the levers and operating a signal, while the former coal office houses a model railway layout. This ride crosses a bridge at Hamsey over the old railway (where the track has been removed), and from The Anchor Inn it follows a section along the trackbed itself (a licensed bridleway, which the landowner allows the public to use) to reach Barcombe Mills station, now a private house. You also cross twice over another line that ran from Lewes to East Grinstead.

Barcombe Mills

Two Roman roads – one from the west and the other from London – once met here. There was a mill here for 900 years until 1939; all that remains are the huge mill pool and gushing weirs. A plaque tells you this was, in 1066, the first place in Sussex

to have a tollgate: look out for the list of tolls by the bridge, showing charges in old money – 's' for a shilling (5p) and 'd' for a penny (12 pennies to the shilling).

the ride

1 With the Royal Oak pub on your right go along the main street in Barcombe and turn left in front of the village sign for **The Anchor Inn and Newick**. At the bottom of the hill turn right on Boast Lane, signposted Anchor Inn. After passing **Delves Farm**, and just before a house on the right, look for a track signposted **'bridleway'** on the left, into a triangular field. At the next triangular area, look to your left for a gate with a yellow arrow on it: at the far end of the field a line of hedgerow trees rising up to the top right skyline marks the line of a Roman road that ran from London to Lewes. Continue along the track, which later follows the left side of a field and passes a wartime **brick pillbox**. The route drops to a **footbridge**. Continue across a meadow to the gate ahead, up over another footbridge and along a track; ignore driveways to the right.

LITTLE HORSTED

At the road T-junction turn right into **Isfield**. Pass the Laughing Fish pub on your left to visit the Lavender Line.

2 From Isfield retrace your route across the meadows and back past the pillbox. Turn left on the road to continue to **The Anchor Inn**.

3 Retrace your route a short distance from The Anchor Inn and, just before **Keeper's Cottage** on the left, turn left on the **old railway track**, signposted 'licensed bridleway to Barcombe Mills'.

4 On reaching a road opposite the old **Barcombe Mills station**, detour left and take the first road on the left. Turn right at the junction in front of the driveway to **Barcombe House** to reach the millpond and weirs of **Barcombe Mills**. Return the same way to the road, past **Barcombe Mills station**. At the next junction go straight ahead for a short-cut back into Barcombe. For the main route, turn left here, and pass

Isfield Station on the Lavender Line

3h00 — **12 MILES** — **19.3 KM** — **LEVEL 1 2 3**

SHORTER ALTERNATIVE ROUTE

1h00 — **4 MILES** — **6.4 KM** — **LEVEL 1 2 3**

MAP: OS Explorer 122 South Downs Way: Steyning to Newhaven

START/FINISH: Barcombe village centre; roadside parking; grid ref: TQ418157

TRAILS/TRACKS: back lanes, hard stony track; optional extension along a track and through fields that get muddy after rain

LANDSCAPE: farmland and river, with distant views of the South Downs

PUBLIC TOILETS: none; when open, Barcombe Mills station has toilets

TOURIST INFORMATION: Lewes, tel: 01273 483448

CYCLE HIRE: Lifecycle, The Tile House, Preston Park, Preston Road, Brighton tel: 01273 542425 (www.lifecyclebrighton.com)

THE PUB: The Anchor Inn, Barcombe

❶ One short climb after Barcombe Mills, otherwise more gentle ups and downs. Take care on blind bends

Getting to the start

Barcombe is signposted from the A26 and A275, 4.3 miles (7km) north of Lewes.

Why do this cycle ride?

Along this route of quiet lanes you'll find everything from Roman sites to wartime defences. Off-road sections follow a disused track, with distant views of the South Downs, and an ancient 'green lane' that crosses fields and leads to the Lavender Line preserved railway.

Researched and written by: Tim Locke

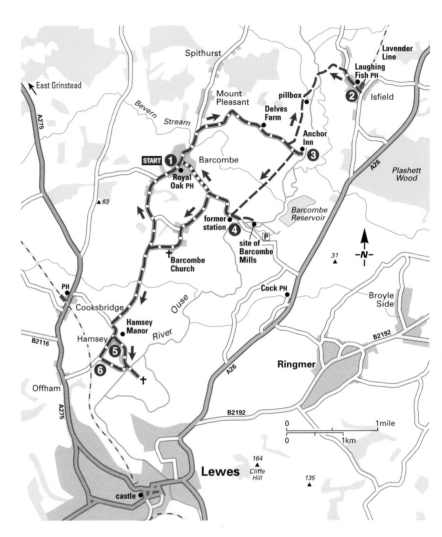

Barcombe church. Carry on along the road, keeping left at the next two junctions towards Hamsey.

5 Just after **Hamsey Manor** turn left down Whitfeld Lane to Hamsey. There is a lovely half-timbered house called **Yeoman's** dated 1584; just after, turn left at a T-junction. The road crosses a former canal via a bridge. After the bridge, you can pick up the keys to **Hamsey church** from **Pine Barn,** the first house on the left. The road rises over the old railway to reach Hamsey church, a wonderful example of what medieval country churches used to look like. Return to **Hamsey,** keep left at the road junction by the **canal bridge,** past a pillbox.

6 Turn right at the T-junction, and after **Whitfeld Lane** joins from the right follow signs for Barcombe to return to the start of the ride.

The Anchor Inn

The white-painted Anchor, built in 1790 mainly to cater for the bargees, has an idyllic location in an isolated spot on the west bank of the River Ouse. It lost its liquor licence in 1895, after the landlord was convicted of smuggling, and didn't regain it until 1963. Refurbished after serious flooding in 2000, the interior features wood and flagstone floors, a warm décor, open fires and a welcoming atmosphere. The big attraction here is the large riverside decking area with views directly to the river and the open countryside beyond. The pub also has 27 boats available for hire by the hour.

Food

Expect classic pub food such as baked trout, cottage pie, chilli, lasagne and various steaks. There are also good snacks and daily specials.

Family facilities

The Anchor Inn has a children's licence so youngsters are welcome anywhere in the pub. There is a basic children's menu and smaller portions of adult dishes are offered. The large front garden is ideal for children; take care by the river.

about the pub

The Anchor Inn
Anchor Lane, Barcombe
Lewes, East Sussex BN8 5BS
Tel: 01273 400414
www.anchorinnandboating.co.uk

DIRECTIONS: The Anchor Inn is at the end of Boast Lane (which becomes Anchor Lane), all by itself, and signposted from the centre of Barcombe village

PARKING: 100

OPEN: daily; all day Easter to September; all day Saturday and Sunday only October to Easter. Phone for winter weekday opening times

FOOD: no food Sunday evening in winter

BREWERY/COMPANY: free house

REAL ALE: Harveys Best, Badger Tanglefoot

ROOMS: 3 rooms (1 en suite)

Alternative refreshment stops

The Royal Oak in Barcombe and the Laughing Fish in Isfield both serve pub food and have gardens. Cinders Buffet at Isfield Station has good-value snacks and light lunches.

☞ Where to go from here

About 4.3 miles (7km) south of Barcombe, Lewes Castle (www.sussexpast.co.uk) stands at the high point of the hilly, ancient town of Lewes. Your entrance ticket includes Barbican House Museum, with its scale model of 19th-century Lewes. The town of Lewes itself is fun to explore, with its many tiny lanes and paths.

The Cuckoo Trail around Hailsham

Well-signposted tracks and lanes link together to create a cycle-friendly ride along a railway track and through peaceful countryside to Michelham Priory.

The Cuckoo Trail

Part of the National Cycle Network, this well-signposted and popular route follows a former railway for most of its 11 miles (17.7km) between Heathfield and Polegate, with an extension to Eastbourne. The railway opened in 1880, linking Polegate with Eridge, and got its name because of a Sussex tradition that says the first cuckoo of spring was always heard at Heathfield Fair. The line closed in 1968, but was revived imaginatively in 1990 as a cycle path, shared with walkers. Quirky iron sculptures and carved wooden benches punctuate the route. Signposted by a former station, the Old Loom Mill complex has a café, crafts, playground, bike hire and the MasterPiece Studio where you can paint your own pottery and collect the results after firing a day or so later.

Michelham Priory

Despite its name, this is a Tudor mansion, set in England's longest medieval, water-filled moat and approached through a 14th-century gatehouse. Wander around the grounds and you will find a physic herb garden with plants that were used for medicine and cooking, re-created Iron Age huts, and the remains of the original priory, where Augustinian canons once lived and worshipped. Inside the house are tapestries, kitchen equipment and an 18th-century child's bedroom; by the entrance is a working watermill which grinds flour for sale.

the ride

1 From the car park, return along the main **driveway** to the road. Turn left and keep left at the first junction. Just after the next junction, turn left on to **Robin Post Lane**, and follow the **'cycle route 2'** signs. The surfacing ends after **New House Farm** on the right. Continue on a track, turning right at the next junction signposted **Cuckoo Trail/route 2**; you can see the South Downs away to the right in the distance.

The Cuckoo Trail has several unique sculptures along its route

Michelham Priory is actually a Tudor mansion with the remains of the original priory

2 At the end of the forest, where there is a house away to the right, ignore a track to the left but keep forward on **cycle route 2**. Beneath the embankment of the A22 turn right on a cycle path, following **Cuckoo Trail signs** which lead you under the main road and along the right side of a road. Avoid crossing a footbridge over the **A27** Polegate bypass and continue on the cycle path. At the next bridge turn left on the **Cuckoo Trail** and follow for 3 miles (4.8km) to Hailsham. The Cuckoo Trail itself is very well signposted and easy to follow. It follows the old railway track for much of the way, but occasionally diverts along small and quiet residential roads. Cross over via **traffic lights**. Later the Trail leaves the old railway track briefly and you enter **Freshfield Close**; follow the Cuckoo Trail signs to right and then to the left.

3 The Trail follows a road close to a **duck pond** and the small park surrounding it, then just after the Railway Tavern on the right it turns left to leave the road, passing close to a **skateboard ramp**. Going under a bridge, it continues along the old railway track. After some playing fields appear on the right, the Cuckoo Trail bends left into a **housing estate**, then right and left on a **path**.

4 Go under **Hawk's Road bridge** and turn left up the ramp, signposted **Michelham Priory**. Turn right on the road, then forward at the mini-roundabout to follow **Hempstead Lane**.

3h15 — **11 MILES** — **17.7 KM** — **LEVEL 1 2 3**

SHORTER ALTERNATIVE ROUTE

3h00 — **9.5 MILES** — **15.3 KM** — **LEVEL 1 2 3**

MAP: OS Explorer 122, South Downs Way: Newhaven to Eastbourne

START/FINISH: Abbot's Wood car park; grid ref: TQ558072

TRAILS/TRACKS: largely compacted gravel and earth tracks, muddy in places; some quiet back lanes and residential roads

LANDSCAPE: woodland, farmland, railway track, suburban roads

PUBLIC TOILETS: at the start

TOURIST INFORMATION: Eastbourne, tel: 01323 411400

CYCLE HIRE: MP Cycle Hire (passed on the Cuckoo Trail), the MasterPiece Studio, Old Loom Mill, Ersham Road, Hailsham BN27 4RG, tel: 01323 449245 or 07974 443119

THE PUB: The Old Oak Inn, Arlington

❶ Often muddy for a short section after Point 5. Use the bike crossing point on the A22 at the edge of Hailsham, and take special care as this road is usually busy

Getting to the start

Abbot's Wood car park is signposted from the A27 between Lewes and Polegate. Take the north turn (Thornwell Road), signposted Arlington and Abbot's Wood. Keep left at the first road junction and right at the next junction, then soon turn right at the signpost to Abbot's Wood car park.

Why do this cycle ride?

The ride uses the Cuckoo Trail and is easy to cycle as most of it is on a disused railway track.

Researched and written by: Tim Locke

Hailsham EAST SUSSEX

5 At the **A22** dual carriageway, cross very carefully by the traffic islands indicated with blue bicycle/pedestrian symbols, and take the lane signposted to **Michelham Priory** opposite. The road surfacing ends by the last cottage on the left, and the lane continues as an often rather muddy track. Just after the track bears left, ignore a bridleway forking right, and continue along to a road. Before turning right along the road, you can detour left for a short distance to have a look at the entrance to **Arlington Stadium**, a venue for stock-car racing and speedway.

6 At the next junction detour right to **Michelham Priory**, then right again at the access road to the Priory itself. Return to the previous road junction and turn right towards Arlington and Wilmington, past **The Old Oak Inn**. Take the next left to return to Abbot's Wood car park.

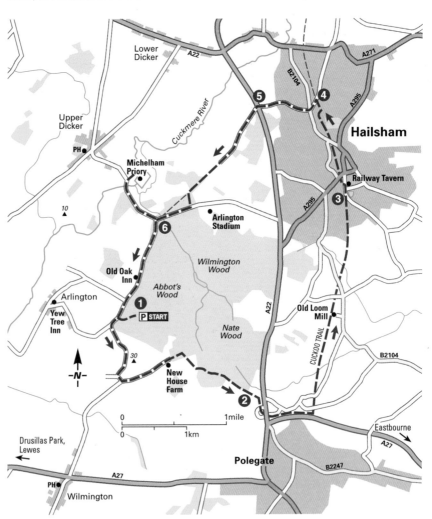

The Old Oak Inn

Built in 1733 as the village almshouse, the Old Oak became a pub in the early 1900s and supplied ale and cider to the workers in the local brick-making and charcoal-burning industries. The friendly, open-plan bar has big beams, blazing winter log fires, comfortable seating and a relaxed atmosphere. Ales are tapped from the cask and you will find a good choice of time-honoured pub games to while away an hour or two on inclement days. In sunny weather head out into the secluded rear garden and savour the South Downs views.

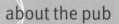

about the pub

The Old Oak Inn
Arlington, Polegate
East Sussex BN26 6SJ
Tel: 01323 482072

DIRECTIONS: follow directions to Abbots Wood car park (above), go past Abbots Wood for 0.5 mile (0.8km) and it's on the left side of the road

PARKING: 40

OPEN: daily; all day

FOOD: daily; all day Saturday and Sunday

BREWERY/COMPANY: free house

REAL ALE: Harveys Best, Badger Best, changing guest beers

Food

The menu offers light meals such as ploughman's salads and filled baguettes. More substantial dishes include 'Oak Favourites' like ham, egg and chips, home-made fishcakes and a large Yorkshire pudding filled with Cumberland sausage and rich gravy. Alternatives range from the daily curry and mixed grill to blackboard specials like seafood gratin and lamb shank in minted gravy.

Family facilities

Children of all ages are welcome inside. There are high chairs, children's portions of main menu dishes, a menu for young children and a wooden adventure frame and slide in the garden.

Alternative refreshment stops

The Railway Arms in Hailsham has a children's area in the garden, and there's a café with a playground at Old Loom Mill on the Cuckoo Trail and a café for visitors at Michelham Priory.

☞ Where to go from here

Four miles (6.4km) south west of Abbot's Wood, Drusillas Park (www.drusillas.co.uk), on the road to Alfriston, has a wonderful animal collection. Animals are kept in conditions similar to those they would experience in the wild. There are monkeys, meerkats, a farmyard area, and 'Penguin Bay' with underwater viewing points, plus play areas, a miniature railway and a paddling pool.

Friston Forest and Cuckmere Haven

Three wonderful contrasts: the Cuckmere river, as it meanders its way to the sea, the tranquil greenery of Friston Forest, and the sweeping views from the top of the South Downs.

Cuckmere Haven

The winding Cuckmere River ends at Cuckmere Haven, the only undeveloped estuary in Sussex, where there is a glorious view along the bottom of the Seven Sisters to the left and the cottages on Seaford Head to the right. The beach is shingle and shelves quite steeply, so this is for stronger swimmers only. During the war, a mock town with lights was built here to mislead enemy bombers into raiding this instead of Newhaven; there are still fortifications here, including concrete 'dragon teeth' tank traps seen to the right, just before the beach. The meadows, reed beds and ponds are important habitats for wildlife. As you approach the beach you will pass an artificial lagoon, made in 1975, and a nesting and feeding area for birds.

Friston Forest and Westdean village

The forest was planted in the early 20th century over an underground reservoir: at some points on the route you can see the waterworks and water tower. Westdean is a secluded village surrounded by the forest. Next to the church stands a rectory dating from the late 13th century.

Above right: A family day out along safe paths

the ride

1 From the car park go down towards the vehicular entrance, and just before the road turn right on a track signposted '**public bridleway to Westdean**'. Look out for the bicycle symbols in green, which denote the bike trail you will be following for the first part of the ride.

2 On reaching the first house at Westdean keep forward on the cycle track (signposted **Exceat Hill**), following the green bike symbols. After 1 mile (1.6km) reach a junction marked with five tall red-and-white posts.

3 For a short return to **Westdean**, fork left almost immediately after, and continue following the **green bike symbols**, turning right at the hard forest road (to the left you can see the tall **red and white posts**), then soon left at another bike symbol. The track rises (at the top a short path leads up right to a **viewpoint** over the forest and to the sea) and then falls. Leave the waymarked trail at a three-way fork, keeping right downhill, past a barrier and houses, then turn right at a road junction into Westdean. Pass the **church** and rectory and drop to a T-junction by **Pond Cottage**, then go ahead towards the flight of steps, where you turn right along the track you were following earlier and retrace to the start.

For the main route, continue ahead at Point 3 and fork left near some **power lines**. Go past a barrier, and forward again on joining a metalled road, which becomes less surfaced (ignore side turns). On reaching a road, turn left along it to **Jevington**. Note the blue plaque on the

<table>
<tr><td>4h00</td><td>12 MILES</td><td>19.3 KM</td><td>LEVEL 123</td></tr>
</table>

SHORTER ALTERNATIVE ROUTE

<table>
<tr><td>2h00</td><td>7 MILES</td><td>11.3 KM</td><td>LEVEL 123</td></tr>
</table>

MAP: OS Explorer 123, South Downs Way: Newhaven to Eastbourne

START/FINISH: Seven Sisters Country Park pay car park (on north side of A259; grid ref: TV518995

TRAILS/TRACKS: well drained, compacted earth and forest tracks, level concrete track to Cuckmere Haven; short downhill road section, steep rough tracks and two stony descents on the long ride

LANDSCAPE: forest, riverside, shingle beach, open chalk downland

PUBLIC TOILETS: at the start

TOURIST INFORMATION: Eastbourne, tel: 01323 411400

CYCLE HIRE: The Cuckmere Cycle Company (by Visitor Centre), tel: 01323 870310; www.cuckmere-cycle.co.uk

THE PUB: The Plough and Harrow, Litlington
❶ Cycle carefully and give pedestrians on the track to Cuckmere Haven priority at busy times. The full ride on the South Downs Way is unsuitable for younger children

Getting to the start
From the A259 between Eastbourne and Seaford, turn off at Seven Sisters Country Park, behind the visitor centre, and immediately turn right for the car park.

Why do this cycle ride?
On this route you will find deep, varied forest laced with cycle paths, and a level, easy ride to the shingle beach at Cuckmere Haven for a famous view of the Seven Sisters.

Researched and written by: Tim Locke

Friston Forest

EAST SUSSEX

Hungry Monk restaurant, informing you this was the birthplace of banoffee pie in 1972.

4 Turn left at Jevington and take the track signposted **South Downs Way** and church: inside there is a 1,000-year-old stone carving of Christ stabbing a beast (AD 950), the triumph of Good over Evil. Continue uphill on the South Downs Way, which steepens through the woods (too steep for cycling). Ignore side turns.

5 At the top, emerge from the **woodland**, ignore the South Downs Way to the right and keep forward. There are wonderful views inland and towards the sea from this track, and just to the left is **Lullington Heath Nature Reserve,** where there is an unusual combination of plants because of the acidic conditions on the chalky soil. The track later drops steeply and then rises up to a junction by a small **flint pillar** on the left. Slightly hidden to the right is **Winchester's Pond**, a small pond that is the haunt of dragonflies.

Friston Forest EAST SUSSEX

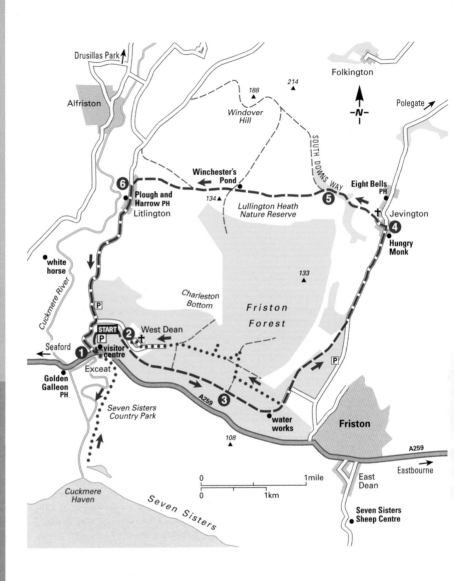

Carry on ahead and downhill, forking left later to **Litlington**, where the track twists left and then right by **farm buildings**.

6 At the road, turn left through Litlington, past the tea gardens and **The Plough and Harrow** pub. You will soon see the figure of a **white horse** etched into the hillside across the valley. The road leads back to the turning to Westdean and the car park at Exceat. To extend the ride, wheel your bike between the restaurant and **visitor centre** on a brick path to the main road. Cross very carefully and take the gate opposite, near the bus stop. The concrete track leads towards the **sea**. Keep right at two forks, following a bicycle route to the **beach**. Return the same way you came.

The Plough and Harrow

Gloriously situated on the edge of the South Downs, this extended 15th-century brick-and-flint pub stands in sleepy Litlington in a secluded spot in the Cuckmere Valley. Original wattle-and-daub walls and a large open fireplace in the small original building hint at the pub's old age, while the carpeted, low beamed lounge and 'railway dining-car' restaurant in the more modern extension are tastefully furnished. There is a sun-trap front garden and an attractive rear lawn with smart benches and umbrellas for summer drinking.

Food
The good, wholesome pub fare served in this attractive pub includes ploughman's lunches, home-made pies (steak and Harveys stout), fresh battered cod, roast belly of pork, and Sussex smokies – smoked haddock, cream and potatoes with cheese topping.

Family facilities
Children are very welcome inside and there's a children's menu available.

about the pub

The Plough and Harrow
Litlington, Alfriston
East Sussex BN26 5RE
Tel: 01323 870632

DIRECTIONS: the pub is on the full ride; if you are following the short ride, load up your bikes and turn right out of the car park to get there, or cycle there (an easy 1.6 miles/2.5km each way). It is on the left of the road, near the church

PARKING: 50

OPEN: daily; all day Saturday and Sunday

FOOD: daily

BREWERY/COMPANY: free house

REAL ALE: Harveys Bitter, Badger Tanglefoot, guest beer

Alternative refreshment stops
Exceat Farmhouse Restaurant (by the visitor centre) serves meals and snacks. You can also try Litlington Tea Garden in Litlington, the Eight Bells, Jevington, just off route, or the Golden Galleon at Exceat, just west of the start, via the A259.

☛ Where to go from here
South east from Exceat is the Seven Sisters Sheep Centre (www.sheepcentre.co.uk), one of the world's largest collections of sheep, with many rare breeds and other farm animals. Visit the Clergy House in Alfriston (www.nationaltrust.org.uk), or visit Drusillas Park (www.drusillas.co.uk), one of the best small zoos in the country.

Friston Forest EAST SUSSEX

A loop from Pevensey to Herstmonceux

A journey between two castles, through the lonely expanse of the Pevensey Levels in '1066 Country'.

A tale of two castles

Pevensey Castle (www.english-heritage.org.uk) has the distinction of being in use for over 1,600 years. In the 4th century the Romans built the large outer

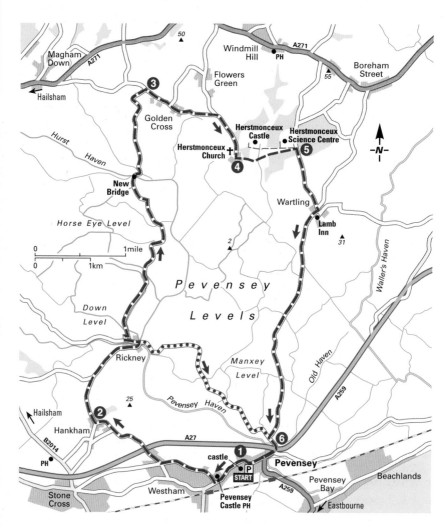

Pevensey   EAST SUSSEX

wall you can see from the road. A public footpath leads through the arch from the corner of the road, allowing a view of the Norman castle erected by William the Conqueror, which has an impressively gloomy dungeon, and remains of the keep and chapel. It was attacked many times after the Norman Conquest, and the walls have collapsed at all sorts of odd angles. In the 1940s, during World War II, it was used as a defence again, and you can see fortifications on the walls. Back in 1076 coins were minted in Pevensey on the site of the 14th-century Mint House, now an antiques shop. It was used as a hideaway by smugglers and is believed to be haunted.

The domes of the former Royal Greenwich Observatory house the lively Herstmonceux Science Centre (www.the-observatory.org), where you can experience science 'hands on', peering through a microscope, investigating the forces of gravity or touring the telescopes. You can turn your energy into electricity to make a model train run, try out the Bouncing Balls or feel the vibrating effect of the Magic Bowl.

the ride

1 From the car park, go to the main street in Pevensey and turn left along it, passing the outer wall of the **castle** (you can walk in through the gateway, where there is free access, if you don't intend to visit the castle fully later). Just after the **Pevensey Castle pub** turn right along Peelings Lane, ignoring a minor turn soon on the left. Turn right at a crossroads and follow signs to **Hankham**.

2h30 — **13 MILES** — **20.9 KM** — **LEVEL 1 2 3**

SHORTER ALTERNATIVE ROUTE

1h00 **5.5 MILES** **8.8 KM** **LEVEL 1 2 3**

MAP: OS Explorer 124 Hastings and Bexhill
START/FINISH: Pevensey car park (by castle; pay and display); grid ref: TQ646048
TRAILS/TRACKS: all on minor roads, except for an earthy bridleway at Herstmonceux (well-drained but uneven surface, and stepped for a short distance; necessary to push your bike); the short ride is on roads
LANDSCAPE: wetland, waterside, farmland
PUBLIC TOILETS: at the start
TOURIST INFORMATION: Eastbourne, tel: 01323 411400
CYCLE HIRE: MP Cycle Hire, the MasterPiece Studio, the Old Loom Mill, Ersham Road, Hailsham BN27 4RG, tel: 01323 449245
THE PUB: The Lamb Inn, Wartling
🅛 0.75 mile (1.2km) off-road section at Herstmonceux may be muddy and includes steps, where you will have to push. Take care crossing the roundabout outside Pevensey

Getting to the start
Pevensey is just west of the A27 and A259 junction, east of Eastbourne.

Why do this cycle ride?
They may be flat, but the Pevensey Levels are full of colour, character and wildlife, while the South Downs rise dramatically in the background. The ride connects the two contrasting castles at Pevensey and Herstmonceux via a winding, almost traffic-free lane, then a wider road leads down to Wartling and across the Levels to Pevensey.

Researched and written by: Tim Locke

Pevensey **EAST SUSSEX**

Pevensey

EAST SUSSEX

The ruined towers of Pevensey Castle's west gate.

note the mounting block for horse-riders outside. Have a look inside for the tomb of Thomas Lord Dacre (died 1553) and his son Sir Thomas Fiennes. There are also two life-sized marble effigies of knights in armour (not the two Thomases), one with his feet resting on a bright red bulldog, which has a gold crown for a collar.

4 Past the church, where the public road ends, go forward, veering left on the bridleway, and follow blue arrows and waymarkers for the **1066 Country Walk**. This leads over a surfaced area near college outbuildings and a car park, and down through **woodland** (it can be muddy). It then crosses a field, with an excellent view of **Herstmonceux Castle** to the left, a superb brick moated castle begun in 1441 with a gatehouse topped by two towers; it is not always open to the public, so enjoy the view from here. Ahead is one of the **telescope buildings** of the former Royal Greenwich Observatory, from whose atomic clocks the familiar six-pips were originally transmitted to the BBC for broadcast. The observatory, which had to move from Herstmonceux because there was too much light pollution, is now based in the Canary Islands. You need to push your bike up some steps and later you will see the other domes of the **old observatory** (now Herstmonceux Science Centre).

5 Turn right on the road (just to the left is the entrance to the Science Centre and Herstmonceux Castle and grounds) and cycle down to Wartling, keeping right in front of **The Lamb Inn**. Continue cycling ahead for 2.5 miles (4km) back to the edge of Pevensey.

6 Cross the **roundabout** carefully, using the cycle crossing points, and take the road into Pevensey to return to the cycle ride start point.

2 Turn right at a T-junction in Hankham, signposted **Rickney**. Keep right at the next junction for Rickney (**National Cycle Route 2**). For a short loop back, at the next junction (in Rickney itself) turn right, then right after 1.5 miles (2.4km). Cross the roundabout and take the road back into **Pevensey**.

For the main ride, turn left at the junction in Rickney (signposted **Hailsham**), then take the first right, signposted **Herstmonceux**. Both the short and full rides have lovely views across the Pevensey Levels, which was once sea. The area eventually filled with shingle, and in medieval times was reclaimed to make farmland. Now it is an important wetland with many bird and flower species.

3 After 3 miles (4.8km) turn right at the next junction and keep right at two more junctions to reach **Herstmonceux Church**;

The Lamb Inn

The 17th-century Lamb Inn underwent extensive refurbishment in 2003 and now draws discerning pub-goers across the marshes for imaginative pub food, good wines and a civilised atmosphere. Beyond the chatty locals' bar, with its wood-burning stove, there's a beamed snug bar, with a brick fireplace and old wooden tables topped with chunky church candles. More candles and flowers decorate the smart lounge, where you can relax in deep sofas and armchairs while studying the interesting, weekly changing blackboard menu before dining in the spacious, yet cosy, warmly decorated restaurant.

Food

Local produce is a feature of the menu, which includes loin of local cod with olive tapenade and pesto mash, Seaford Bay scallops and pancetta, and shank of South Downs lamb with mint and red wine gravy. Further choices are home-made burgers and pies, sausage and mash, confit of duck, tasty soups and puddings such as chocolate bread and butter pudding.

about the pub

The Lamb Inn
Wartling, Herstmonceux
East Sussex BN27 1RY
Tel: 01323 832116
www.lambinnwartling.co.uk

DIRECTIONS: on the road between Pevensey and the A269 (from the A269, turn off just east of Windmill Hill, signposted Pevensey and Wartling)

PARKING: 22
OPEN: daily; not Sunday evening
FOOD: daily; not Sunday evening
BREWERY/COMPANY: free house
REAL ALE: Harveys Best, guest beers

Family facilities

Children are allowed in the eating area of the bar and there's a children's menu available. The super back terrace has flower tubs, a pond and fountain.

Alternative refreshment stops

Castle Cottage Restaurant, next to the entrance to Pevensey Castle, and there are The Smugglers and Pevensey Castle pubs in Pevensey.

☛ Where to go from here

Eastbourne (www.eastbourne.org/tourism), is a handsome seaside resort. The Museum of Shops has a collection of 100,000 shop items. The Miniature Steam Railway Park features one-eighth-scale steam and diesel trains that take you round a lake.

Pevensey EAST SUSSEX

From Winchelsea to Rye and beyond

Two historic gems, and a castle in between, plus the biggest and best sandy beach in the south east.

Winchelsea and Rye

Today Winchelsea seems an idyllic sleepy village, yet in medieval times it was one of the prosperous 'Cinque Ports' – Channel port towns that supplied ships and men to the navy. It was built in the 13th century in a grid plan after the old town at the foot of the hill was washed away in a storm. Black Death and attacks from the French led to lean times over the next two centuries, and much of it was rebuilt later on; many

houses still have vaulted cellars (some visible from the street) for storing wine, and there are three town gateways. The church stands partly incomplete, partly ruined, but inside it is grandly proportioned, with fine canopied tombs. Visit the Court Hall Museum for the full story.

Similarly lost in time, Rye was another Cinque Port, stranded inland as the sea has receded. Its knot of hilly streets, including cobbled Mermaid Street with its ancient Mermaid Inn, has a delightful array of tile-hung, timber-framed and brick buildings. The Landgate and Ypres Tower are medieval fortifications, and don't miss the glorious view from the top of the church tower. The Rye Castle Museum looks at the town's past.

The cobbled road and plant-festooned buildings in Rye's Mermaid Street

the ride

1 With the New Inn on your left and the churchyard behind you, take the road ahead to the **A259 sign**, turn right towards Rye and soon descend steeply. Take the first left, signposted **Winchelsea Station**, as the road hairpins sharp right. After the level crossing (stop and wait if the light is red), turn right at the T-junction on **Dumb Woman's Lane**. As the road starts to bend left uphill take the bridleway through the gate ahead (signposted **National Cycle Route 2**). This goes along the foot of what used to be sea cliffs in Roman times.

2 Turn right by a **pumping station** (with green turrets), avoiding the road ahead near houses, on a permissive cycle path to reach **Gibbet Marsh car park**. Keep right to skirt the car park (if you are starting from here, take the path at the back of the car park, near the **picnic benches**, and turn left). The path bends right, opposite a **windmill**, and crosses the railway line. You will later return to Winchelsea by following the road to the right, but first go left and round to the right into **Rye town centre**, wheeling your bike through town. Visit the tourist information centre/Rye Heritage Centre/Town Model, then turn left and go up cobbled **Mermaid Street**. Turn right at the top along West Street, then right and left to skirt the right side of the churchyard. In front of Ypres Tower, turn left, then right, soon passing **Rye Castle Museum**. Turn right at the next junction, and just before

3h30	9 MILES	14.5 KM	LEVEL 123

SHORTER ALTERNATIVE ROUTE

2h30	5 MILES	8 KM	LEVEL 123

MAP: OS Explorer 125 Romney Marsh

START/FINISH: New Inn, Winchelsea (free roadside parking near the pub and church); grid ref TQ904174. Alternative start: Gibbet Marsh car park, Rye; grid ref: TQ915203

TRAILS/TRACKS: roads, surfaced cycle paths, stony in places, grass track: mountain bikes recommended

LANDSCAPE: farmland, coast

PUBLIC TOILETS: Winchelsea, Rye, Camber Sands

TOURIST INFORMATION: Rye, tel: 01797 226696

CYCLE HIRE: Rye Hire, Rye, tel: 01797 223033; Sundays and bank holidays tel: 01797 227826

THE PUB: The New Inn, Winchelsea

🛑 Short sections on main road. Take care with road crossings in Winchelsea and Rye. Cross the railway with care at Winchelsea Station and at Rye. Wheel your bike through Rye when going in the Camber direction. One steep hill up into Winchelsea

Getting to the start

Winchelsea is signposted off the A259 between Rye and Hastings. You can also start at Rye: use Gibbet Marsh car park signposted from the B2089.

Why do this cycle ride?

Apart from the little hills on which the Rye and Winchelsea stand, this is a level route from Winchelsea to Camber Sands, and a more demanding close to Camber Castle.

Researched and written by: Tim Locke

Winchelsea EAST SUSSEX

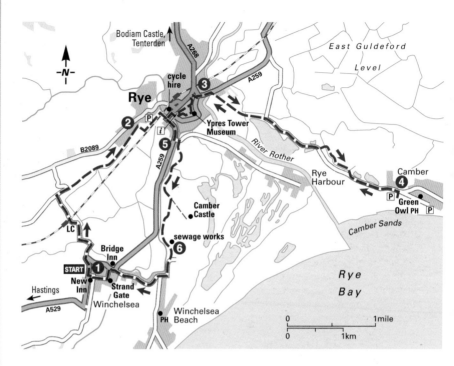

the **town gate** (Landgate), turn right at the end of the railings, go down a path and over a zebra crossing, then left through the car park and right through the park to join the pavement by the **A259**.

3 At a **bike symbol** you can now ride your bike again, along the pavement and over the A259 river bridge. Turn right on the other side on the **bike path**, signposted to Camber. This later crosses the road by a traffic island. After 2 miles (3.2km) the bike path ends by **houses**.

4 Cross the road, enter the car park and take the path over the dunes and on to **Camber Sands**. Return the same way to Rye: wheel your bike over the zebra crossing and up the path to the Landgate. Cycle left along Rye's main street, ignoring side turns, and drop downhill to reach a junction of roads. Take the road ahead (the continuation of Mermaid Street) to reach the **tourist**

information centre. Wheel over the zebra crossing away to your right and follow the A259 towards **Hastings** (either cycling along the road or wheeling your bike along the pavement).

5 Turn left, signposted **Rye Harbour**, over the canal, then turn right on a bridleway. At the next house, fork left through a gate. The route follows a raised **grassy dyke**. At a junction near **concrete sheds**, with Camber Castle ahead, keep right in the direction of the blue arrow (or leave your bike here and walk along the path to see the castle). The track is fainter and bumpier, following a slight ridge.

6 By a **sewerage works** join a concrete road, then keep forward along a tarmacked road. Turn right on a larger road, left on the A259, and left up a steep road into **Winchelsea**. Go under Strand Gate and keep forward to reach **The New Inn**.

The New Inn

The comfortably old-fashioned 18th-century New Inn is opposite the church in the centre of this ancient town. The cosy, rambling interior has three bustling beamed rooms, all sporting nice old furnishings and good warming winter log fires. There's a separate locals' bar, well-kept Greene King ales and simply furnished bedrooms with delightful views. An inviting walled garden to the rear of the pub is perfect for alfresco meals or simply to relax in following an energetic walk or cycle ride.

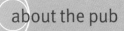

about the pub

The New Inn
German Street, Winchelsea
East Sussex TN36 4EN
Tel: 01797 226252

DIRECTIONS: The New Inn is opposite the church in the middle of Winchelsea

PARKING: 20

OPEN: daily; all day

FOOD: daily; all day Sunday

BREWERY/COMPANY: Greene King

REAL ALE: Greene King IPA and Old Speckled Hen, Morland Original

ROOMS: 6 en suite

Food

You can order home-made pies, roast chicken, a range of steaks with sauces, and hearty snacks such as sandwiches and ploughman's lunches from the printed menu. The specials board includes local fish such as whole Dover sole and red mullet alongside lamb shank in red wine, and minced beef and onion pie.

Family facilities

Well-behaved children are allowed in the bar area and restaurant, where young children can choose from a standard kids' menu.

Alternative refreshment stops

There's the Tea Tree (tea room) and the Bridge Inn at Winchelsea, plus a full range of cafés, restaurants, pubs and shops in Rye, and cafés and the Green Owl pub in Camber.

☛ Where to go from here

Fifteen miles (24.1km) north west of Rye is Bodiam Castle (www.nationaltrust.org.uk), a fairytale, 14th-century ruin surrounded by a moat. The walls stand to their original height, and there are staircases and turrets to climb. You can reach it by riding a steam or diesel train on the Kent and East Sussex Railway (www.kesr.org.uk) from just outside Tenterden, a rewarding little Wealden town with many weatherboarded houses.

From Bushy Park to Ham

Mingle with the deer in the second largest royal park.

Cobbler's Walk

On this ride you follow Cobbler's Walk for about a mile (1.6km). The path gets its name from a memorial at the Hampton Wick Gate of Bushy Park which tells the story of local shoemaker Timothy Bennet. In 1752 he noticed that people no longer passed his shop on their way to Kingston Market from the west because they had to go the long way round by the road. Bushy Park's ranger Lord Halifax had closed the path through the park. Bennet's principle in life was that he was 'unwilling to leave the world worse than he found it' so he decided to do something about the closure of the path, and set about consulting an attorney with a view to establishing a public right of way through the park. He served notice of action on Lord Halifax, who was

unimpressed with Bennet's impertinence and immediately dismissed the claim. On reflection, the earl began to see that the claim might have some foundation, and – fearing public defeat by a mere shoemaker – withdrew his opposition. As a result the pathway is enjoyed by the public to this day and now bears the name Cobbler's Walk.

the ride

1 From the car park head west past the 'no entry' signs. Remain on the **main surfaced road** when Cobbler's Walk diverges to the left. When the road turns sharply left, bear right to exit Bushy Park. Continue through the gate to reach **Hampton Road**.

2 Cross Hampton Road and pick up **King's Road** opposite, taking the first right at Connaught Road. At Gloucester

A track through Bushy Park

3h00 — **8 MILES** — **12.9 KM** — **LEVEL 123**

MAP: OS Explorer 161 London South

START/FINISH: Bushy Park; Cobbler's Walk car park; grid ref: TQ153701

TRAILS/TRACKS: mix of gravel paths, surfaced traffic-free trails and roads

LANDSCAPE: riverside, parkland and suburban streets

PUBLIC TOILETS: Canbury Gardens, Kingston

TOURIST INFORMATION: Kingston upon Thames, tel: 020 8547 5592

CYCLE HIRE: none available locally

THE PUB: The Bishop Out of Residence, Kingston upon Thames

❶ Some sections are shared with traffic; those with very young children may prefer to dismount

---

Road, turn left then right at Stanley Road. Beyond the bus stop turn left into Somerset Road, with a quick right turn into Stuart Grove, which becomes Sutherland Grove then Walpole Crescent. Turn right into Church Road to reach **Broad Street**.

3 At the traffic lights turn left to cross the railway bridge and join Teddington High Street. When the high street becomes Ferry Road look out for the **Landmark Arts Centre** on the right, housed in the imposing former St Alban's church. Cross the main road and continue along Ferry Road to the lock.

4 Dismount at the lock to cross the **double footbridges**. Once on the far bank of the river continue straight ahead to reach Riverside Drive. Cross the road and pick up the **cycle path** opposite to reach Hardwicke Road. Simpson Road and Broughton Avenue lead to Lock Road;

Getting to the start

The Cobbler's Walk car park is reached from Chestnut Avenue, which runs north–south through Bushy Park. The Park is reached from Kingston via the A308 Hampton Court Road.

Why do this cycle ride?

This ride is a voyage of discovery, from the village atmosphere of Ham Common to the market town of Kingston and the expanse of Bushy Park. Spot some of the 350 red and fallow deer in the park, introduced by Henry VIII for hunting.

Researched and written by: James Hatts

Bushy Park SURREY

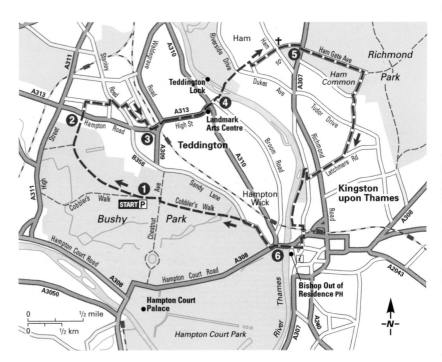

at the **Catholic church** continue straight ahead along Ham Common to reach the A307 (Upper Ham Road/Petersham Road).

5 Cross straight over (with care) into **Ham Gate Avenue**, where there is a traffic-free cycle track parallel to the road. Just before Ham Gate take a left turn down Church Road. When the road forks, bear left along Latchmere Lane. Continue for about 0.5 mile (800m) to reach Latchmere Road, bearing right to reach Richmond Road. Take care crossing here to pick up Bank Lane. At Lower Ham Road turn right to skirt the edge of Canbury Gardens and pick up the **riverside path** heading south. Just before the railway bridge head inland along Down Hall Road and follow the **signed cycle route** through Kingston town centre to cross Kingston Bridge. (For the pub, turn left down Thames Street just before the bridge, then right into Bishop Hall.)

6 Across the bridge bear left along Hampton Court Road, but take the first right along Church Grove, turning left when this joins Park Road. Enter Bushy Park through Hampton Wick Gate, and bear half-right along Cobbler's Walk, crossing Longford River with Leg-of-Mutton Pond to your left. After 0.5 mile (800m) Cobbler's Walk reaches Chestnut Avenue, a busy road running north–south across the park. Cross the avenue and pick up Cobbler's Walk diagonally opposite back to the car park.

The Bishop Out of Residence

about the pub

The Bishop Out of Residence

2 Bishops Hall, off Thames Street
Kingston upon Thames, Surrey
KT1 1QN
Tel: 020 8546 4965

DIRECTIONS: just below Kingston Bridge; see Point **5**

PARKING: Kingston Fairfield NCP near by

OPEN: daily; all day

FOOD: daily; all day

BREWERY/COMPANY: Young's Brewery

REAL ALE: Young's Bitter, Special and seasonal beers

Built in the 1960s, this is a clean and well-maintained Young's pub in a stunning location right beside the Thames with views across to Hampton Court Park. The small riverside patio makes the most of the view and can get busy on summer weekends, so arrive early. On cooler days, take in the view from the large picture windows in the unpretentious upstairs bar. Rest your weary legs and sink into one of the deep burgundy sofas dotted around the part-carpeted, part-wood-floored room, which has a distinct sailing/rowing theme to its décor.

Food

The traditional pub menu includes various sandwiches, Cumberland sausages and mash, a changing range of home-made pies, and a selection of grills and specials such as beer battered calamari.

Family facilities

Children are welcome in the upstairs bar until 7pm. Keep small children supervised if you are outside at the waterfront tables.

Alternative refreshment stops

You will find a choice of pubs and cafés in Teddington High Street and in Kingston town centre.

☛ Where to go from here

Head across Bushy Park to visit Henry VIII's magnificent Tudor palace at Hampton Court. With over 500 years of royal history it has something to offer everyone, from the sumptuous, richly decorated State Apartments and beautiful gardens to the domestic reality of the Tudor kitchens. Costumed guides and fascinating audio tours bring the palace to life. Or you can explore the extensive riverside grounds which include the famous Maze, laid out in 1714 and still puzzling most who enter (www.hrp.org.uk).

Richmond to Ham House

An easy riverside circuit that is ideal for all ages.

Ham House

Built in 1610, Ham House is best known as home to the flamboyant Duchess of Lauderdale, whose relentless political scheming was at the heart of Civil War politics and Restoration intrigue. Some claim that the Duchess still haunts the house today. The garden is gradually being restored to its 17th-century splendour. The Orangery houses a tea room, which offers menus inspired by the gardens, such as lavender syllabub, using lavender grown in the famous Ham cherry gardens, and locally made sausages cooked in apple and onion gravy, flavoured with sage from the Ham gardens.

Quarries once occupied the site of what is now Ham Lands Nature Reserve. These were filled in after World War II with rubble from London buildings destroyed in the blitz. The variety of soils from all over the capital has created a unique pattern of different vegetation types attracting many unusual species.

the ride

1 From Water Lane head down the hill to the riverside. Wheel your bike along to **Richmond Bridge**. Beyond the bridge the towpath runs alongside a narrow strip of parkland parallel with **Petersham Road**. Soon **Buccleugh Gardens** is reached and the path moves briefly inland.

1h30 — **5.5 MILES** · **8.8 KM** — **LEVEL 123**

MAP: OS Explorer 161 London South

START/FINISH: Watermans Arms, Water Lane, Richmond; grid ref: TQ176747

TRAILS/TRACKS: largely compacted gravel and surfaced tracks

LANDSCAPE: riverside

PUBLIC TOILETS: in Buccleugh Gardens

TOURIST INFORMATION: Richmond, tel: 020 8940 9125

CYCLE HIRE: Roehampton Gate, Richmond Park, tel: 07050 209249

THE PUB: Watermans Arms, Richmond

🛑 Some rough unsurfaced riverside sections

Richmond SURREY

Getting to the start

The Watermans Arms is in Water Lane, a cobbled street that runs between the main post office and the river. It is approached via Red Lion Street in the town centre's one-way system. Richmond Riverside car park is just to the west of Water Lane.

Why do this cycle ride?

A fairly gentle yet fulfilling circular ride based in the busy shopping and cultural centre of Richmond, taking in the village of Ham. Discover what happened to the rubble from the World War II Blitz on London.

Researched and written by: James Hatts

2 The path returns towards the river to skirt the edge of **Petersham Meadows**. Continue straight ahead at the **River Lane slipway**. This section of the path can be slightly rough.

3 At **Hammerton's Ferry** head inland across the boardwalk. Take the bridleway which runs alongside **Ham House**. At the end of the first section bear diagonally right to pick up **Melancholy Walk**. Look at the view back to the house behind you, then cross Sandy Lane and continue straight on till the path emerges at **Ham Common**.

Above: Following the River Thames to Richmond Hill
Right: The Jacobean architecture of Ham House

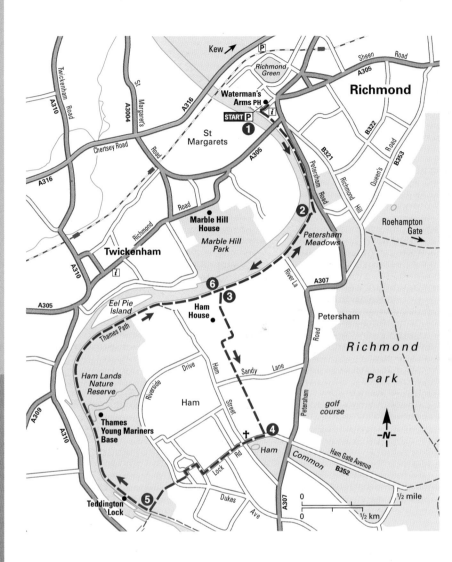

4 Turn right at **Ham Common** and keep straight ahead along Lock Road. At the end turn right into Broughton Avenue, left into Simpson Road and left into Hardwicke Road. Follow the cycle signs for the alleyway to reach Riverside Drive and the approach to **Teddington Lock**.

5 At the footbridge turn right and join the **riverside path**. Pass the locks which

mark the limit of the tidal Thames. Soon you come to **Thames Young Mariners Base**; cross the bridge here and enter the **Ham Lands Nature Reserve**. Ham House is once again revealed, just past Eel Pie Island.

6 From Ham House return to **Richmond** via your outward route.

Watermans Arms

The signs in Water Lane proclaim the wonders of the Watermans all-day breakfast, but the speciality at this traditional, single-bar pub is its Thai menu. Tucked down a narrow cobbled lane leading to the Thames, it's an unpretentious little pub, noted locally for its friendly atmosphere and its genuine, unspoilt feel, and is a good place to escape the crowds that descend on the larger, more prominent riverside pubs. The décor reflects the pub's associations with the Thames – note the boat suspended from the ceiling in the bar. Arrive early in summer to secure one of the outside tables.

Food

If Thai food isn't to your taste, there's a range of burgers, chips, sandwiches and baguettes. A traditional roast is served on Sunday lunchtimes.

Family facilities

Children are welcome inside the pub.

Alternative refreshment stops

There are plenty of bars, cafés and restaurants to choose from in Richmond.

☞ Where to go from here

Visit Marble Hill House, a magnificent Thames-side Palladian villa set in 66 acres (26ha) of riverside parklands in Twickenham. It contains fine examples of early Georgian painting and furniture (www.english-heritage.org.uk). Explore the magnificent conservatories at Kew Gardens and discover plants from the world's deserts, mountains and oceans (www.kew.org). Or why not stay in Richmond and learn more about the history of the town at the Museum of Richmond (www.museumofrichmond.com).

about the pub

Watermans Arms
10 Water Lane, Richmond
Surrey TW9 1TJ
Tel: 020 8940 2893

DIRECTIONS: see Getting to the start
PARKING: Richmond Riverside Car Park, just to the west of Water Lane
OPEN: daily; all day
FOOD: daily; all day
BREWERY/COMPANY: Young's Brewery
REAL ALE: Young's Bitter, Special and seasonal beers

Kingston upon Thames to Hampton Court

A traffic-free riverside ride to one of Britain's most famous royal palaces.

Hampton Court Palace

The palace is often associated with Henry VIII, who in just ten years spent more than £62,000 (equivalent to £18 million today) rebuilding and extending Hampton Court. At the time of his death, Henry had more than 60 houses and Hampton Court was his fourth favourite; he spent 811 days here during his 38-year reign, and all of his six wives came to the palace. The story of Hampton Court goes back to the early

Above: Kingston Bridge
Left: Traffic-free cycling

| 2h00 | 7 MILES | 11.3 KM | LEVEL 123 |

1200s, when the site was first occupied by the Knights Hospitallers of St John of Jerusalem. For another royal occupant of the palace, however, it was later to become a prison – Charles I was held here for three months. George II was the last monarch to use the palace fully; his heir George III didn't much care for Hampton Court, remarking after a fire in some outbuildings that he 'should not have been sorry if it had burnt down'. The palace was opened to the public by Queen Victoria in 1838. Today, besides the palace itself, the world-famous maze and the Great Vine (planted in 1768) continue to delight thousands of visitors every year.

the ride

1 From **The Boaters Inn** turn south along the shady riverside path. Just before the railway bridge follow the **signed cycle route** to the left along Down Hall Road. Turn right at Skerne Road and follow the cycle track under the railway bridge. Use the cycle crossing provided to cross **Wood Street**. Take the buses-and-cyclists-only section of Wood Street round the side of the Bentall Centre, following round to reach the crossroads with Clarence Street. Turn right to approach **Kingston Bridge** using the clearly marked cycle lane.

2 Cross the bridge on the segregated **cycle path** and turn left along the riverside. Keep to the surfaced track known as **Barge Walk**.

MAP: OS Explorer 161 London South
START/FINISH: The Boaters Inn, Canbury Gardens, Kingston upon Thames; grid ref: TQ179702
TRAILS/TRACKS: largely compacted gravel, with some surfaced sections
LANDSCAPE: riverside
PUBLIC TOILETS: Kingston upon Thames
TOURIST INFORMATION: Kingston upon Thames, tel: 020 8547 5592
CYCLE HIRE: none available locally
THE PUB: The Boaters Inn, Kingston upon Thames
❗ Give way to pedestrians on the shared riverside path

Getting to the start

From Seven Kings car park in Skerne Road go up Down Hall Road, alongside the railway, and head north to the Boaters Inn via the riverside path. The Boaters Inn is in Canbury Gardens, 0.5 mile (800m) north of Kingston Bridge on the eastern bank of the river. Lower Ham Road runs parallel to the A307 Richmond Road. There are pay-and-display car parks in Kingston upon Thames town centre.

Why do this cycle ride?

This is a straightforward ride suitable for all ages and links the pleasant market town of Kingston upon Thames with the familiar landmark of Hampton Court Palace via the excellent riverside path.

Researched and written by: James Hatts

3 Soon the watersports centre and yacht club of **Raven's Ait** (an island in the river) is reached. Remain on the riverside path.

4 **Thames Ditton Island**, with its 48 houses, is the next major landmark on the river. **The Pavilion**, designed by Sir Christopher Wren, is on the towpath here. When the surfaced track resumes you are now on **Pavilion Terrace**. Follow the brick wall of Hampton Court Park; soon views of the Broad Walk will emerge. Closer to the palace the path gets wider and will be busy on a fine summer's day.

5 The ride ends at **Hampton Court Bridge**; you may wish to explore the Palace and grounds before returning to Kingston by retracing your outward route.

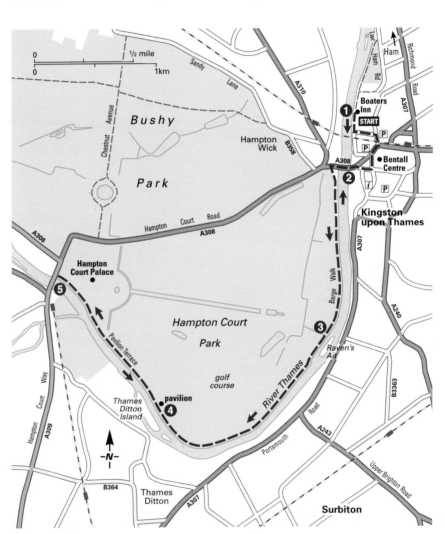

The Boaters Inn

The key to this modern pub's appeal lies in its splendid riverside location, with fine views of the busy Thames. There are moorings provided for those arriving by boat and the 10 per cent discount for rowers demonstrates that this waterside pub takes its river connections seriously. Colourful hanging baskets brighten the façade in summer, and the popular outdoor tables benefit from the shade of large trees in the adjacent Canbury Gardens. The Boaters is known locally for its live jazz and blues nights.

Food

Instead of conventional starters and main courses, the menu is divided into 'small plates' and 'big plates'. From the former you can order Cajun potato wedges and dip or deep-fried brie with fruit sauce; from the latter Thai green curry and various fish, pasta and burger meals. Puddings include chocolate profiteroles, summer pudding and ice cream.

Family facilities

Children are welcome inside the bar. Facilities include a children's menu and baby-changing facilities.

Alternative refreshment stops

Choose from the pubs and cafés at Hampton Court.

☞ Where to go from here

Spend time exploring Henry VIII's magnificent Tudor palace at Hampton Court. Costumed and audio tours bring 500 years of history alive (www.hrp.org.uk). Visit Ham House, a fine Stuart house built in 1610 in beautiful gardens beside the

about the pub

The Boaters Inn
Canbury Gardens, Lower Ham Road
Kingston upon Thames, Surrey
KT2 5AU
Tel: 020 8541 4672

DIRECTIONS: see Getting to the start; the pub is beside the Thames

PARKING: pay-and-display in Kingston town centre

OPEN: daily; all day

FOOD: daily; all day

BREWERY/COMPANY: free house

REAL ALE: Greene King IPA, Shepherd Neame Spitfire, Adnams Broadside

Thames, containing an original collection of fine 17th-century furniture (www.nationaltrust.org.uk). Alternatively, stay local and discover more about the history of the town at the Kingston Museum (www.kingston.gov.uk/museums).

Around Richmond Park

Discover the capital's largest open space and enjoy amazing views of the city.

Richmond Park

At 2,500 acres (1,012ha) Richmond Park is Europe's largest urban walled park, which has an abundance of wildlife in its varied landscape of hills, woodland gardens and grasslands. Charles I brought his court to Richmond Palace in 1625 to escape the plague in London and turned it into a park for red and fallow deer. There are more than 750 deer in the park today. Pembroke Lodge was the home of Lord Russell, prime minister in the mid-1800s. His grandson Bertrand Russell grew up here. The restaurant that now occupies the building enjoys spectacular views of the Thames Valley. The Isabella Plantation is a stunning woodland garden that was created in the early 1950s from an existing woodland and is organically run, resulting in a rich flora and fauna. Over 1,000 species of beetle have been recorded in the park. The ancient oaks provide a rich habitat for many types of insect. The park enjoys the status of a Site of Special Scientific Interest and a National Nature Reserve.

the ride

1 On entering the park at Richmond Gate look for the path on the left-hand side. (From Pembroke Lodge car park return to Richmond gate and turn right.) The path skirts **Bishops Pond**. Keep straight on past Cambrian Gate. Adam's Pond is to your right just beyond **East Sheen Gate**. The bridge over Beverley Brook means you are nearly at **Roehampton Gate**.

2
At Roehampton Gate cross the road. The path continues past the café and car park, where cycle hire is available. The **golf course** is to your left. Soon the path crosses Beverley Brook once again, then it remains between the brook and the park road as far as **Robin Hood Gate**.

3
At **Broomfield Hill** the steepest ascent of the ride awaits; signs advise cyclists to dismount. There is a bench at the top where you can recover, and a well-placed r**efreshment kiosk** is just beyond. The Isabella Plantation is to your right. At **Kingston Gate** the route starts heading north.

4
At **Ham Gate** the path crosses the road and turns right, ascending

A busy stretch of the ride through Richmond Park

1h30	7 MILES	11.3 KM	LEVEL 1 2 3

MAP: OS Explorer 161 London South

START/FINISH: Richmond Gate at Richmond Park; grid ref: TQ184737

TRAILS/TRACKS: largely compacted gravel

LANDSCAPE: parkland and woodland

PUBLIC TOILETS: around the park

TOURIST INFORMATION: Richmond, tel 020 8940 9125

CYCLE HIRE: Roehampton Gate, tel 07050 209249

THE PUB: Lass O'Richmond Hill, Richmond

❶ Some short, steep climbs and a couple of longer ascents through woodland

Getting to the start
Richmond Gate is at the top of Richmond Hill (B321). You can approach from Richmond town centre or if you are coming from the south leave the A307 at Star and Garter Hill. There's parking at Pembroke Lodge in the park.

Why do this cycle ride?
This is an enjoyable circuit on an easy traffic-free trail shared with pedestrians. The stunning views of St Paul's Cathedral and other London landmarks are the only reminders that you are just 10 miles (16.1km) from the centre of the capital.

Researched and written by: James Hatts

Richmond Park SURREY

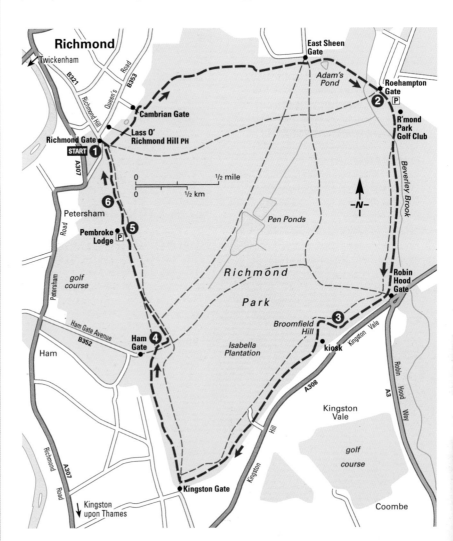

parallel to the road. At the T-junction turn left, remaining parallel to the road. Soon the path leaves the road and opens on to a wide tree-lined avenue. As you approach **Pembroke Lodge**, glorious views of the Thames Valley unfold to the left.

5 At Pembroke Lodge the path is sometimes congested with pedestrians. Just beyond Pembroke Lodge, with the

barrow known as **King Henry VIII's mound** on your left, the cycle path unexpectedly moves to the right. At this point a marker beside the path draws attention to the incredible view of **St Paul's Cathedral**, 10 miles (16.1km) away.

6 As you ride on, a panoramic view of other London landmarks opens out. Before long you will be back at **Richmond Gate**.

Richmond

↖ Twickenham

B321

Richmond Hill

Queen's Road

B353

Cambrian Gate

Lass O' Richmond Hill PH

Richmond Gate

START **1**

A307

6

Petersham

Pembroke Lodge P **5**

Petersham Road

golf course

Ham Gate Avenue

B352

Ham

Ham Gate 4

Richmond Road

A307

↓ Kingston upon Thames

Kingston Gate

Kingston Hill

Kingston

Isabella Plantation

Broomfield Hill

kiosk

Kingston Vale

A308

Kingston Vale

golf course

Coombe

East Sheen Gate

Adam's Pond

Roehampton Gate P **2**

R'mond Park Golf Club

Beverley Brook

Pen Ponds

_-N-_

Richmond _Park_

Robin Hood Gate

3

Robin Hood Way

A3

0 ___ ½ mile
0 ___ ½ km

74

Lass O'Richmond Hill

Perched high on the steep Richmond Hill this pub is ideally placed for a cycle ride around the park. The sign outside promises 'home cooked food all day, every day, 8 days a week'. The fully air-conditioned interior means that this is a pleasant place to spend time in all weathers, and the main bar is spacious and airy. Abundant window boxes and hanging baskets add a colourful touch to the exterior. There are a few tables on the pavement, but the small garden terrace to the rear is a quieter and more pleasant place to eat and drink on sunny days.

Food

Menus change every three months and may include starters such as smoked salmon, chef's sardines and Welsh rarebit. Main courses include chicken stuffed with asparagus and chef's special fillet steak with gnocchi. Traditional apple pie and chocolate truffle tart are among the puddings. There are also daily chalkboard specials to look out for.

about the pub

Lass O'Richmond Hill
8 Queens Road, Richmond
Surrey TW10 6JJ
Tel: 020 8940 1306

DIRECTIONS: on Queen's Road (B353), just to the northeast of Richmond Gate
PARKING: 25 spaces
OPEN: daily; all day
FOOD: daily; all day
BREWERY/COMPANY: Chef & Brewer
REAL ALE: Courage Best, Fuller's London Pride, Bombardier

Family facilities

Children are made welcome and there's a children's menu for younger family members.

Alternative refreshment stops

There are various cafés in the park and at Pembroke Lodge.

☞ Where to go from here

You're spoilt for choice for places to visit after your ride. Head off to Kew Gardens and explore some of the 3,000 acres (1,215ha) and the magnificent conservatories filled with exotic plants (www.kew.org). Take the children to Twickenham Stadium for a behind-the-scenes look at the home of England rugby and Britain's top sporting museum, the Museum of Rugby (www.rfu.com).

Richmond Park SURREY

Barnes and Chiswick

A cross-river ride linking two London villages.

Chiswick House

Chiswick House is an attempt to re-create the kind of house and garden found in the suburbs of ancient Rome. It was designed in the 18th century by Richard Boyle, third Earl of Burlington, who employed William Kent to create sumptuous interiors to contrast with the pure white exterior. The historian Sir Kenneth Clark described the house as 'a masterpiece of domestic architecture'. The third Earl was a renowned patron of the arts, supporting writers including Alexander Pope and Jonathan Swift and the composer Handel. Surprisingly the villa was never intended as a residence but a temple of the arts. Two British prime ministers have died at the house, and it has played host to a huge number of international royals and statesmen. The Earl of Burlington paid great

A double staircase and two-storey portico decorate the front of Chiswick House

1h30 · **4 MILES** · **6.4 KM** · **LEVEL 123**

MAP: OS Explorer 161 London South

START/FINISH: The Coach and Horses, Barnes High Street; grid ref: TQ216764

TRAILS/TRACKS: nearly all surfaced tracks and roads

LANDSCAPE: riverside, parkland and streets

PUBLIC TOILETS: none on route

TOURIST INFORMATION: Hounslow, tel: 0845 456 2929

CYCLE HIRE: none available locally

THE PUB: Coach and Horses, Barnes, SW13

🛈 You will need to carry your bike up some stairs to cross a bridge

Getting to the start

Barnes is close to the A205 South Circular Road. The Coach and Horses is in Barnes High Street, close to the river. There is on-street pay-and-display parking in the area.

Why do this cycle ride?

This is a short circular ride linking the London villages of Barnes and Chiswick, taking in the breathtaking Chiswick House and its grounds, as well as offering vistas of the Thames.

Researched and written by: James Hatts

Barnes LONDON

attention to improving the grounds, the features of which include an obelisk, temple, amphitheatre, cascade and wilderness.

the ride

1 Turn left outside the Coach and Horses pub and approach the River Thames. Bear left along the riverside and cycle on until you reach **Barnes Bridge station**. Dismount at this point.

Barnes LONDON

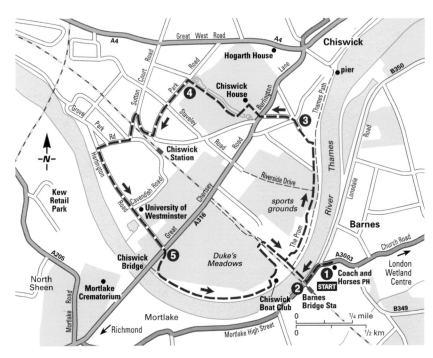

2 Take the stairs here to cross **Barnes Bridge**. On the far side of the bridge descend the steps. Do not follow the riverside path; turn left and head inland a short distance to reach a wider, surfaced track. Turn right here along **The Promenade** and pass the bandstand and other sports ground amenities. Where **Riverside Drive** turns sharply inland, continue straight ahead by the river. Notice the unusual sculptures here. When **Chiswick Pier** is in sight and you reach the cycling prohibited signs, bear inland up the long lane to the roundabout.

3 At the roundabout bear left towards the off-licence and take the right-hand fork along Grantham Road. Cross Burlington Lane to enter **Chiswick House Grounds**. Observe any signs restricting cycling in this area. Head straight on towards the entrance to **Chiswick House**. By the gates, turn left to cross the bridge by the **cascades**. Turn right

up the side of the lake and exit the grounds on to **Park Road**.

4 Turn left along Park Road and keep straight ahead at Staveley Road. On reaching **Chiswick Station**, turn right along Sutton Court Road. Take a sharp left turn to cross the railway on **Grove Park Bridge**. Take the second right along Grove Park Road. At Hartington Road turn left, then beyond Cavendish Road, the **University of Westminster**'s sport ground looms on the left.

5 Cross **Great Chertsey Road** (the approach to Chiswick Bridge) and pick up the lane on the other side that loops round towards the river and skirts **Duke's Meadow**. The track eventually wiggles inland around Chiswick Boat Club. Soon the track dives under the **railway**; turn right here and return to Barnes Bridge. Cross the bridge and return to the south bank of the Thames.

Coach and Horses

First leased by Young's Brewery in 1831, this fine old coaching inn retains plenty of character and its unassuming frontage doesn't betray what lies behind it. A narrow archway leads to a long beer garden, with a boules pitch and small play area at the very rear. Behind the stained glass lies a small, cosy bar filled with a cast of regulars who create a friendly, welcoming atmosphere. Furnishings are traditional and décor includes St George's flags draped around the bar, photographs of Barnes in days gone by lining the walls, and a selection of books to peruse while enjoying a pint of Young's Special.

Food

A barbecue counter in the garden serves traditional fare such as sausages and burgers throughout the summer. A more conventional menu is also available, with the usual hot dishes and a range of ploughman's meals.

Family facilities

Children are welcome in the Family Room. There's a family dining room if the weather is inclement, while on sunny days children can enjoy the play area in the garden.

about the pub

Coach and Horses
27 Barnes High Street, Barnes
London SW13 9LW
Tel: 020 8876 2695

DIRECTIONS: on the south side of Barnes High Street, between the village centre and the river

PARKING: on-street pay and display

OPEN: daily; all day

FOOD: daily; all day

BREWERY/COMPANY: Young's Brewery

REAL ALE: Young's Bitter, Special and seasonal beers

Alternative refreshment stops

There are various pubs and cafés in Barnes and Chiswick.

☞ Where to go from here

Just along the road is the unique, state-of-the-art Wildfowl and Wetlands Trust Centre, set in 105 acres (42.5ha) of wild wetlands. Here you can explore lakes and marshes, view birds and animals from multistorey hides and learn more about wildlife at the interactive Discovery Centre (www.wetlandcentre.org.uk). Don't miss out on a visit to Chiswick House along the route (www.english-heritage.org.uk). In Chiswick, just off the A4 in Hogarth Lane, you can visit Hogarth House, once home to the artist William Hogarth (1697–1764), to view displays on the artist's life and many of his satirical engravings.

Wimbledon Common and beyond

Discover some of south west London's hidden villages.

Wimbledon Windmill

A popular local landmark, the windmill was built in 1817 to serve local residents who didn't trust the 'factory produced' flour from the large mills on the River Wandle. The mill's working life ended in 1864 when Earl Spencer, the lord of the manor, announced his intention to enclose Wimbledon Common and build a new manor house on the site of the mill. Local opposition led to a six-year legal battle, resolved by the 1871 Wimbledon and Putney Commons Act, which handed over the common to the local community. The mill was then converted into homes for six families. Robert Baden-Powell, founder of the Scout movement, lived at the adjacent Mill House for a time and wrote part of *Scouting for Boys* here. A museum opened in the windmill in 1975; more recently Lottery funding has enabled the sails to be restored to working order. The museum tells the story of windmills around the world, including early Persian and Greek examples, as well as modern wind farms. An information centre with general information on Wimbledon and Putney Commons is a short distance from the windmill.

the ride

1 From Southside Common take the short cycle lane north along **The Green**, which almost immediately turns on to the common, with **Rushmere Pond** to the left. Soon the gravel path crosses Cannizaro Road before converging at the junction between West Side Common and The Causeway. Turn left here along **Camp Road**,

Left: Wimbledon Common
Below: Wimbledon Windmill

1h30 — **7.5 MILES** — **12.1 KM** — **LEVEL 123**

MAP: OS Explorer 161 London South
START/FINISH: Southside Common, Wimbledon Village; grid ref: TQ237710
TRAILS/TRACKS: mixed; some well-surfaced paths, some rough tracks
LANDSCAPE: woodland, parkland and suburban streets
PUBLIC TOILETS: at gates of Richmond Park
TOURIST INFORMATION: Richmond, tel: 020 8940 9125
CYCLE HIRE: Smith Brothers, 14 Church Road, Wimbledon, tel: 020 8946 2270
THE PUB: Fox & Grapes, Wimbledon Common, SW19 4UN
🛈 Some rough unsurfaced sections; may be muddy after heavy rain

---

Getting to to the start
Southside Common is just off Wimbledon High Street in Wimbledon Village. There is metered parking around Southside Common.

Why do this cycle ride?
This circuit links three of south-west London's often under-appreciated green spaces: Wimbledon Common, Putney Heath and Richmond Park. There is a marked contrast between the more natural, rural feel to Wimbledon Common and Richmond's carefully managed royal park.

Researched and written by: James Hatts

---

with the **Fox & Grapes** pub to your right. At Camp View, take Sunset Road through the gate signed for **Thatched Cottage**. Close to Springwell Cottage, look for the **gate** to the left, marked for cyclists. Take this path; this section is unsurfaced and involves bouncing over many exposed tree roots. Much of it is also shared with horse riders, so the path can be churned up.

2 When you reach a bridge over **Beverley Brook**, remain on the east bank and turn right. Past the playing fields, turn left across the bridge and head for the footbridge over the main road. Use the toucan crossings here to reach the Robin Hood Gate into **Richmond Park**.

3 Go straight ahead along the park road, then bear right on reaching the car park. There are views across **Pen Ponds** to your left. Here the path is wide and well surfaced. There is a climb up to **White Lodge**, home of the Royal Ballet School. To the left there is a great view along Queen's Ride. The path swoops downhill to the T-junction with Sawyer's Hill; turn right here and join the traffic-free **cycle path** parallel to the road.

4 Leave the park at **Roehampton Gate**, taking the right-hand fork along Prior Lane and the first right into **Danebury Avenue**. There is no through route for motor vehicles, but there is a gap between the bollards for cyclists. Continue past the bus terminus and follow the avenue as it curves round to meet Roehampton Lane. Cross over here and go straight ahead along

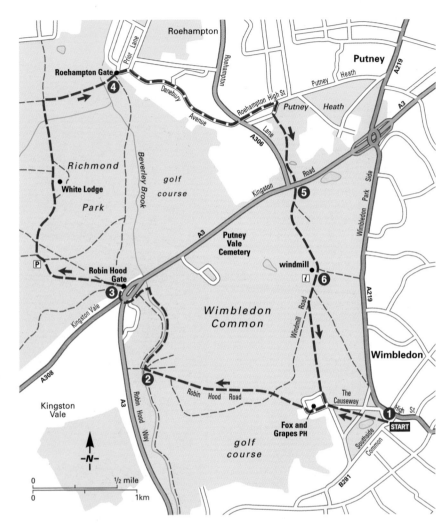

Roehampton High Street. Turn right into Medfield Street and pick up the **cycle path** on to Putney Heath by the war memorial. Beyond **Scio Pond** the path comes close to the A306 before passing underneath the A3 via a subway.

5 Beyond the subway take the right-hand fork (Windmill Road). At the green gate turn right for access to the **windmill**, museum, information centre and tea room.

6 From the windmill go straight ahead through the **green gate**, but keep a good lookout for the left-hand fork. Take this path, which crosses over two horse rides. Soon the path emerges on to the road at **West Place**, with its picturesque cottages. At this point if you are in need of refreshment you can take a right turn into Camp Road for the Fox & Grapes pub or continue straight on to return to **Southside Common** along the outward route.

Fox & Grapes

The Fox & Grapes, which dates back to 1787, looks and feels like a small rural pub, set as it is on the edge of Wimbledon Common. The main bar with its high-beamed ceiling once housed stables in the 18th century, while the original bar to the left is now a smoke-free area with cosy stools and benches. One of the pub's claims to fame is that from 1868 it was used for 20 years as the changing rooms for what later became Wimbledon Football Club. The landlord's enthusiasm for fine wines is reflected in the extensive wine list; ale drinkers will not be disappointed with the Bombardier bitter on tap.

Food

An appetising tapas menu with ingredients sourced from Spain is available all day. You could also try the pub's speciality pork pies, served as a ploughman's lunch and made to a 19th-century recipe, using Gloucester old spot pork.

Family facilities

Children are made very welcome throughout the pub.

Alternative refreshment stops

Try the tea room at Wimbledon Windmill or one of the pubs around Wimbledon Common, including the Crooked Billet and the Hand-in-Hand.

☛ Where to go from here

At the Wimbledon Lawn Tennis Museum (www.wimbledon.org), pictures, displays and memorabilia trace the development of the game over the last century. See the world-famous Championship's trophies,

about the pub

Fox & Grapes
9 Camp Road, Wimbledon Common
London SW19 4UN
Tel: 020 8946 5599

DIRECTIONS: Camp Road can be reached via The Causeway from Wimbledon High Street (A219)

PARKING: on-road metered parking around Southside Common and The Causeway

OPEN: daily; all day

FOOD: daily; all day

BREWERY/COMPANY: free house

REAL ALE: Wells Bombardier

as well as archive film and video footage of great players in action, and enjoy a behind-the-scenes guided tour of Centre Court, No. 1 Court and the press interview room.

From Fulham to Hammersmith

Discover Harrods furniture repository, Fulham football club and a bishop's palace.

Fulham

Fulham Football Club has played at the riverside Craven Cottage ground since 1896. Now with a capacity of 22,200, it continues to play an important part in English football. The team known as 'the Cottagers' returned home for the 2004 season after a couple of years ground-sharing with Queen's Park Rangers. The building, which lends its name to the ground, is a listed structure and can be seen clearly from the cycle route.

Fulham Palace was a residence of the Bishop of London for more than 1,200 years between 704 and 1973, and once boasted the longest moat in England. In its current form it comprises a fascinating mixture of architectural styles, from the red brick of the Tudor courtyard to the elegant Georgian east frontage. Excavations have revealed evidence of neolithic

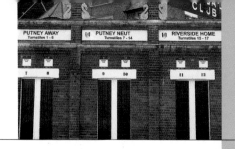

Below left: Fulham Palace, the residence of the Bishops of London until 1973
Left: Fulham football ground

1h30 — **4.5 MILES** — **7.2 KM** — **LEVEL 123**

and Roman settlements on the site. The palace gardens achieved fame in the 17th century when rare species such as the magnolia were imported and grown here for the first time. Today a museum is based in the early 19th-century part of the palace where you can find out about the Palace's history.

the ride

1 Ride upstream from Putney Bridge along **Putney Embankment**. Look out for the 'UBR' bollard marking the start of the annual University Boat Race. Continue past the various boathouses and clubhouses. Towards the end of the surfaced section is **Leader's Gardens**, to the left.

2 The path becomes rough (and muddy at times) beyond the bridge that carries the towpath over **Beverley Brook**. Continue past the Sea Scout headquarters. Barn Elms school sports centre is through the trees to your left and across the river there are views of **Craven Cottage**. Ignore the National Cycle Network route signed to the left and remain on the towpath to Harrods Village and **Hammersmith Bridge**.

3 Pass underneath the bridge and use the ramp on the far side to reach the road level. Cross the river here and take the first right into Worlidge Street. Turn right into Queen Caroline Street to return towards the river and the **Riverside Studios**. After a left turn into Crisp Road, bear left into Chancellor's Road. Take the first right into Distillery Road. Bear right into Winslow Road, and take a left into **Manbre Road**.

MAP: OS Explorer 161 London South
START/FINISH: Putney Embankment; grid ref: TQ240757
TRAILS/TRACKS: unsurfaced tracks, surburban streets
LANDSCAPE: riverside and parkland
PUBLIC TOILETS: in Bishop's Park
TOURIST INFORMATION: Richmond, tel: 020 8940 9125
CYCLE HIRE: London Recumbents, Battersea Park, tel: 020 7498 6543
THE PUB: The Coat and Badge, 8 Lacy Road
❶ Some short, steep climbs and a couple of longer ascents through woodland

Getting to the start
Putney Embankment is to the west of Putney Bridge on the southern bank of the river. If parking at the Putney Exchange car park, turn left into Putney High Street then left at the Lower Richmond Road to reach the start point. Putney is just inside the South Circular Road.

Why do this cycle ride?
This is an easy circuit with lots to see, from the former Harrods Furniture Depository to Fulham Football Club's famous Craven Cottage ground, as well as Fulham Palace, once the residence of the Bishop of London.

Researched and written by: James Hatts

Fulham LONDON

4 Use the **cyclists-only link** between Manbre Road and Rannoch Road. At Crabtree Lane turn right, then bear left into Woodlawn Road.

5 **Queensmill School** is the next landmark to spot; beyond the school take a right into Queensmill Road to get closer to the river; continue along Stevenage Road until you reach **Craven Cottage**.

6 Beyond the football ground enter into **Bishop's Park** on the right-hand side and follow the signed cycle route past **Fulham Palace**. Leave the park through the gate by All Saints Church and ride up the slope to reach **Putney Bridge Approach**. Turn right to cross the bridge and return to the start.

Fulham LONDON

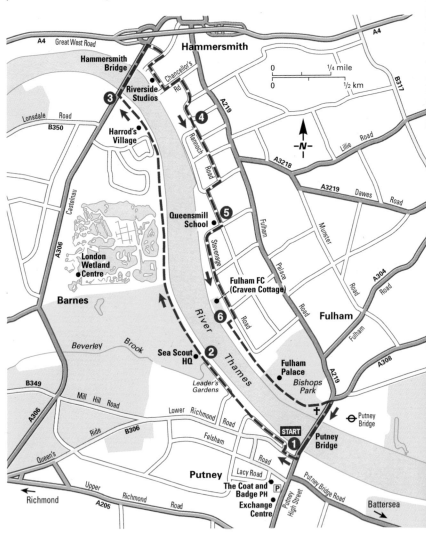

The Coat and Badge

Tucked away in a quiet street, yet just a stone's throw from the bustle of Putney High Street, this light and spacious pub-restaurant offers a civilised retreat from the crowds. The L-shaped room is filled with an eclectic mix of old tables, chairs and relaxing leather settees, bookshelves scattered with books, vases and plants, and warm, yellow-painted walls covered with paintings and objets d'art. The pub has a rowing theme, including a river mural of two rowers, a set of oars and the impressive list of the winners of The Coat & Badge Sculling Race. On warm summer days head for the leafy courtyard garden; in winter relax with a drink in front of the open fire.

Food

The imaginative menu changes monthly and features starters such as smoked haddock cakes with spicy chilli sauce or Caesar salad, followed by Cumberland sausages with parsley mash, fresh pasta and salads, or chargrilled rib-eye steak. There are also daily specials, lunchtime sandwiches and summer barbecues.

Family facilities
Children are welcome before 7PM.

Alternative refreshment stops
You will find a good choice of pubs and cafés in Putney town centre.

☛ Where to go from here
Don't miss the views across the lakes and marshes of the London Wetland Centre on this ride. Why not return and explore it on foot, visit a hide and the informative and interactive Discovery Centre to learn more about the wildlife living here and so close to central London (www.wetlandcentre.org.uk).

Fulham LONDON

about the pub

The Coat and Badge
8 Lacy Road, Putney
London SW15 1NL
Tel: 020 8788 4900
www.geronimo-inns.co.uk

DIRECTIONS: see Getting to the start; the pub is opposite the car park
PARKING: at the Exchange Centre, directly opposite the pub
OPEN: daily; all day
FOOD: daily
BREWERY/COMPANY: Geronimo Inns
REAL ALE: Sharp's, Greene King's

Along the River Wandle

Discover one of London's forgotten rivers.

Merton and Morton

Merton Priory was an Augustinian house founded on the site where the Roman road from London to Chichester crosses the River Wandle. Among those who were educated at the priory were Thomas Becket and the only English pope to date, Nicholas Brakespeare. A church the size of Westminster Abbey once stood on the site now occupied by Sainsbury's Savacentre. After the Reformation the site of the priory became known as Merton Abbey. From the 1660s it became a textile manufacturing centre, and most famously William Morris's calico works were here at Merton Abbey. The Regent Street store Liberty had its printworks here between 1904 and 1972. Several of the buildings are still standing, including the wheel house and water wheel that drove the rinsing spools. The water wheel is still operational and now drives a potters' wheel. Much of the site is occupied by a craft market and farmer's market. The complex is busiest at weekends, but there is plenty to see during the week too.

The estate of Morden Hall Park was created by the Hatfeild family who made their money from snuff milling on the Wandle. Gilliat Hatfeild left the park to the National Trust on his death in 1941. A well-liked philanthropist, Gilliat lived in Morden Cottage rather than the Hall because he considered it better suited to a bachelor. The walled Kitchen Garden, that once required 14 gardeners to maintain it, now houses the car park, garden centre and tea room. Outbuildings such as the tool shed

and boiler house have been converted into workshops for independent craftsmen and women. The National Trust has restored Hatfeild's fine 1922 rose garden, which contains over 2,000 roses.

the ride

1 From The Ship follow the **London Cycle Network** sign for Wandsworth south along Jew's Row past the bus garage. Although cyclists are provided for in the gyratory system, families with small children will prefer to dismount and use the pedestrian crossing to reach old York Road. Pass under the railway bridge at **Wandsworth Town Station** and continue until the traffic lights. Here there is a toucan crossing for pedestrians and cyclists on the right-hand side. Cross over on to Armoury Way and continue until you reach another toucan crossing. Cross here and follow Ram Street, with the **Young's Ram Brewery** on your right.

2 With the **Southside shopping centre** on your right, proceed down Garratt Lane. This is probably the most difficult section of the ride, so you may prefer to push your bike. At Mapleton Road use the toucan crossing, then turn right across the bridge. At the park gates turn sharp left on to the signed cycle trail. The 55-acre (22ha) **King George's Park** was opened by George V in 1923. Spot the unusual blue plaque just before the crossing at Kimber Road. The path now runs between the river and the **adventure playground**. Part of the route is known as Foster's Way, named after Corporal Edward Foster of the 13th Battalion (Wandsworth) of the East Surrey Regiment, who was awarded the Victoria Cross in 1917.

3h00 — **11 MILES** — **17.7 KM** — **LEVEL 123**

3 Leave the park extension through the gates and continue straight ahead along **Acuba Road**. Beware of the confusing cycle route signage here. At Ravensbury Road turn left. Once you have joined Ravensbury Terrace, turn right into Penwith Road and cross the river. At the traffic lights turn right. Again, it is wise to dismount for this section. Once you have passed Earlsfield station turn right into **Summerley Street** at Barclays Bank. When you reach Trewint Street turn right and cross the river, then join the riverside path to the left. At a fork – take the unsurfaced track to the left.

4 At Plough Lane there is a toucan crossing. It is necessary to cross the river as well as the road at this point; the path moves to the east bank. Look out for the metal **Wandle Trail mile marker** on the left. The path is once again well-surfaced and is on a tree-lined embankment high above the water, shaded in summer. Once you have gone under the railway bridge continue straight on with the **Wandle Meadow Nature Park** on your right. The path soon exits on to a concrete road.

5 At North Road turn right, then left at the mini roundabout on to East Road. Once again the signs disappear, so don't miss the right turn at **All Saints Road**. Take a left at Hanover Road and again at Leyton Road. Go past the fire brigade gate and turn left. Use the toucan crossing at Merton High Street. Before the footbridge leading to Savacentre turn right along the riverside path. At the next bridge veer right and head for the small stone arch leading to another toucan crossing at Merantun Way. Cross the road to **Merton Abbey Mills**.

MAP: OS Explorer 161 London South

START/FINISH: The Ship, Jew's Row, Wandsworth, grid ref: TQ259754 or the Southside Centre car park in Wandsworth

TRAILS/TRACKS: largely tarmac paths with some suburban roads and compacted gravel

LANDSCAPE: parkland and waterside

PUBLIC TOILETS: at Morden Hall Park

TOURIST INFORMATION: Merton, tel: 020 8946 9192

CYCLE HIRE: London Recumbents in Battersea Park, tel: 020 7498 6543

THE PUB: The Ship, Wandsworth, SW18

❶ The section between The Ship and King George's Park involves riding on some busy roads

Getting to the start
The Ship and Jew's Row is just off the Wandsworth Gyratory System, south of Wandsworth Bridge. There is on-street metered parking (maximum 4 hours) on Jew's Row. Alternatively, park at the Southside Centre multistorey car park on Garrett Lane in Wandsworth (on the route at Point **2**).

Why do this cycle ride?
This is an enjoyable ride linking the Thames with the beautiful rose gardens of Morden Hall Park, via the industrial heritage of Merton Abbey Mills.

Researched and written by: James Hatts

Wandsworth LONDON

W a n d s w o r t h   LONDON

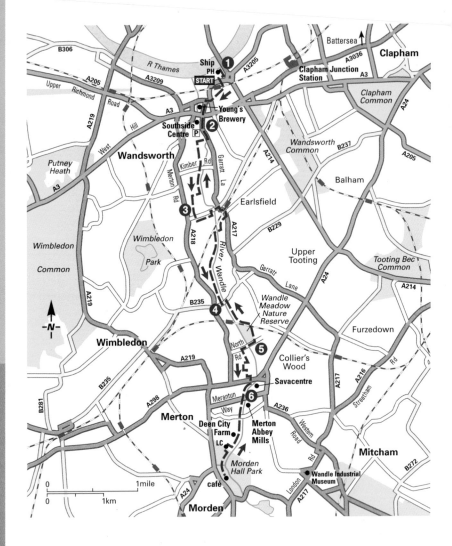

6 Continue past Merton Abbey Mills. At the road bridge cross Windsor Avenue. Here the riverside path doubles as the driveway of **Deen City Farm**. On reaching the farm gate keep straight on past the National Trust sign into **Morden Hall Park**. Turn left at the T-junction to reach a level crossing with the Wimbledon branch of Croydon Tramlink. Soon after the crossing, turn left away from the tramline through the rather unpromising

gap in the fence. This section of the ride runs through the **Morden Hall Park Wetlands,** and a National Trust panel explains the wildlife you are likely to spot. At the next junction turn left and cross two bridges in quick succession. At the larger iron bridge turn right for the National Trust shop and café in the **walled garden** or just explore the park and rose gardens before tackling the return journey.

The Ship

The Ship, next to Wandsworth Bridge on the Thames, exudes a lively, bustling atmosphere. From the road, this 19th-century building has nothing to distinguish it from any other pub, apart from the figurehead above an unused doorway. However, if you approach the pub from the river walk, you will pass through a two-level terrace with a barbecue area and lots of seating, summer bar and colourful trellises and flower boxes, to the attractive, light and airy, conservatory-style lounge bar. Here you will find heavy oak tables and chairs, old desks and even a butcher's table, and there's a central wood-burning stove and an open-to-view kitchen area.

Food

The emphasis of the imaginative menu is on top-quality English produce. Expect the likes of rack of lamb with rosemary and ratatouille, handmade sausages, shepherd's pie, home-made leek and rocket soup and poached haddock with parsley mash.

Family facilities

Children are very welcome inside the pub. Smaller portions are available.

Alternative refreshment stops

There is the William Morris at Merton Abbey Mills and the National Trust Riverside Café at Morden Hall Park.

☛ Where to go from here

On Wandsworth High Street you will find Young's Ram Brewery. Beer has been brewed continuously alongside the River Wandle since 1581 and the present brewery was founded in 1675. You can learn more about the history of Young's and the brewing process at the Visitor Centre, where tours of the brewery (over 14s only) and the stables (over 5s) can be arranged (www.youngs.co.uk). Children will enjoy a visit to Deen City Farm at Merton Abbey, a fascinating community farm where children can learn how to look after animals and plants (www.deencityfarm.co.uk). Secrets of the powerful River Wandle and its industrial past can be explored at the Wandle Industrial Museum in Mitcham (www.wandle.org.uk). For more information about Merton Abbey Mills contact www.mertonabbeymills.com, and for Morden Hall Park www.nationaltrust.org.uk

about the pub

The Ship

41 Jew's Row, Wandsworth
London SW18 1TB
Tel: 020 8870 9667
www.theship.co.uk

DIRECTIONS: see Getting to the start

PARKING: on-street parking in Jew's Row limited to 4 hours on weekdays

OPEN: daily; all day

FOOD: daily; all day

BREWERY/COMPANY: Young's Brewery

REAL ALE: Young's Bitter, Special and Waggle Dance

Wandsworth LONDON

Around Hyde Park

Discover a green oasis in the heart of the capital.

Hyde Park

Henry VIII and his court once hunted deer in Hyde Park; the Tudor monarch acquired the land from the monks of Westminster Abbey in 1536. Public access was first permitted under James I, but it was Charles I who opened the park fully to the general public in 1637. During the Great Plague in 1665 many Londoners set up camp in the park, hoping to escape the disease. The Serpentine – the vast ornamental lake dominating the park – was created in the 1730s by Queen Caroline, wife of George II.

The latest in Hyde Park's long line of royal connections is the controversial £3.6 million Diana, Princess of Wales Memorial Fountain, unveiled by the Queen in 2004. The fountain was designed by US architect Kathryn Gustafson, and is based on an oval stone ring. Water enters the fountain at its highest point, then bounces down steps. It picks up momentum and is invigorated by jets. As it flows westwards it resembles a babbling brook. Air bubbles are added as it approaches a waterfall before entering a water feature. Water from east and west meets at the reflecting pool, before being pumped out to restart the cycle.

the ride

1 From the West Carriage Drive car park, opposite the **Serpentine Gallery**, cross the road and join the cycle track on the pavement on the west side of West Carriage

Safe, traffic-free cycling is possible in Hyde Park in the heart of London

1h00 — **2.5 MILES** — **4 KM** — **LEVEL 1**23

MAP: OS Explorer 173 London North

START/FINISH: West Carriage Drive car park; grid ref: TQ269800

TRAILS/TRACKS: well-surfaced paths

LANDSCAPE: urban parkland

PUBLIC TOILETS: in the park

TOURIST INFORMATION: London Line, tel: 09068 663344

CYCLE HIRE: London Bicycle Tour Company, 1a Gabriels Wharf, 56 Upper Ground, SE1, tel: 020 7928 6838

THE PUB: The Wilton Arms, Kinnerton Street

❗ Be sure to give priority to pedestrians on shared-use paths. Beware of unpredictable rollerbladers!

Getting to the start

The West Carriage Drive car park is south of the bridge over the Serpentine. It can be approached from the A402 Bayswater Road to the north or the A315 Kensington Gore/ Kensington Road to the south. The pay-and-display car park is open 8.30am-6.30pm.

Why do this cycle ride?

An ideal ride for families with very young children, this is a chance to make the most of a huge expanse of green space that Londoners often forget they have on their doorstep. Glance to your left as you cross the Serpentine Bridge and you'd never guess that you were in the heart of the capital. Yet elsewhere there are surprising views of familiar London landmarks.

Researched and written by: James Hatts

Drive. The Diana, Princess of Wales **Memorial Fountain** is on your right.

2 The track drops down on to the road to cross the **Serpentine bridge**. Once across be sure to look out for the point where the path resumes on the pavement, as the cycle lane on the road surface stops abruptly.

3 At Victoria Gate cross the road and follow the cycle path along **The Ring**. The path here is on the road, but it is often traffic-free.

4 As you approach Cumberland Gate and Marble Arch, look for the **cycle route sign** for Chelsea Bridge and cross the road to pick up the cycle path on **Broad Walk**. You may need to reduce speed here

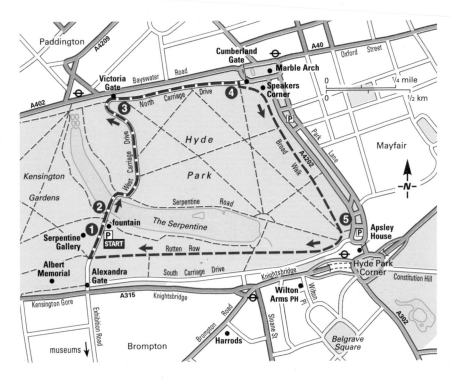

as the cycle lane can be obstructed by crowds milling around at **Speakers' Corner**. It then heads south on Broad Walk, a pleasant, wide, tree-lined boulevard.

5 On the approach to **Queen Elizabeth Gate** at Hyde Park Corner, follow signs to the right for **Rotten Row** to return to the car park at West Carriage Drive. If heading for **The Wilton Arms** pub, you will need to leave the park through this gate. On Rotten Row, keep to the left on this fairly narrow path shared with pedestrians and rollerbladers. At West Carriage Drive, use the pedestrian crossing and pick up the cycle track again on the west side in front of the **Serpentine Gallery**. (This simple circular cycle ride can be easily extended eastwards with a foray along **Constitution Hill**'s excellent parallel cycle track, which would enable a view of Buckingham Palace, or with a jaunt to the west to explore Kensington Gardens. Notices at the park entrances show where cycling is permitted.)

The Serpentine in Hyde Park

The Wilton Arms

Exuberant hanging baskets and window boxes decorate this early 19th-century pub, and a tasteful conservatory occupies the garden, so arrive early to ensure a seat in summer. Inside, high settles and bookcases create cosy individual seating areas, all fully air-conditioned. Owned by Shepherd Neame, Britain's oldest brewer, it was named after the 1st Earl Wilton and is known locally as the 'Village Pub'.

Food

The chalkboard menu lists the house speciality – a doorstep sandwich of salt roast beef with horseradish and mustard dressing. There's also beef and Guinness pie, fish and chips, lamb hotpot and a choice of curries, alongside staples such as burgers and ploughman's meals.

Family facilities

Children are welcome inside the bar if they are eating, and smaller portions of main menu dishes can be ordered.

Alternative refreshment stops

You will find various cafés and kiosks in Hyde Park.

☞ Where to go from here

Along the ride, stop off at Apsley House, The Wellington Museum at Hyde Park Corner, the 19th-century home of the first Duke of Wellington. From West Carriage Drive you are within walking distance of the South Kensington museums. Spend some time at the Victoria and Albert Museum (www.vam.ac.uk), the Natural History Museum (www.nhm.ac.uk) or the Science Museum (www.sciencemuseum.org.uk). Explore Kensington Gardens and visit the restored Kings Apartments in Kensington Palace (www.hrp.org.uk). The Serpentine Gallery has fascinating changing exhibitions of contemporary art (www.serpentinegallery.org).

about the pub

The Wilton Arms
71 Kinnerton Street
London SW1X 8ED
Tel: 020 7235 4854

DIRECTIONS: tucked away behind Knightsbridge and best accessed from Wilton Place. From the Queen Elizabeth Gate of Hyde Park, leave the park and cross to the other side of Knightsbridge. Turn right, and continue until you reach Wilton Place. Turn left here, and take the next right. You will soon spot the pub

PARKING: none

OPEN: daily; all day

FOOD: all day; no food Sunday

BREWERY/COMPANY: Shepherd Neame

REAL ALE: Shepherd Neame Goldings, Spitfire and Master Brew

From Battersea to Putney

Battersea LONDON

Discover the delights of Thames-side London.

Battersea Park

It may not look very big on the map, but packed within its relatively small space there is much to see and do in Battersea Park. It attracts a wealth of wildlife; waterfowl regularly spotted on the lake include herons, cormorants, grebes and black swans. The park hosts a variety of cultural events, including a programme of outdoor concerts on summer evenings. There is also a funfair in summer. The Pump

Battersea Park – a haven among London's busy streets

House Gallery is housed in a restored Grade II-listed building, built in 1861 to supply water to the lakes and cascade of Battersea Park. Derelict for many years, it was restored and reopened in the early 1990s as a shop, park information centre and art gallery. Sports facilities are also on offer. London Recumbents offer a chance to try out their unusual cycles on the park's wide avenues, or you can hire a conventional bike to explore further afield.

A close-up view of the Pagoda in Battersea Park

3h30 · **9 MILES** · **14 KM** · **LEVEL 123**

the ride

1 From Rosary Gate head north up **Carriage Drive East**, with the deer enclosure and lake to your left. At The Parade turn left and ride along the wide traffic-free road; the Pagoda is to your left. Leave the park through Albert Bridge Gate and cross Albert Bridge Road to pick up Parkgate Road opposite – **The Prince Albert** pub is on the corner. At Battersea Bridge Road take a diagonal left along Westbridge Road. Look carefully for Granfield Street and turn left. Before you reach the college, look for the signed cycle route and turn right down an unpromising alleyway. This brings you into **Battersea High Street**; turn left here. Just beyond the railway turn right into Gwynne Road and take the first left into **Yelverton Road**.

2 Cross York Road on the crossing and pick up Wye Road on the other side. By the church follow the bend round into Ingrave Street. This turns into Fowler Court. At Plough Road turn left, and very soon pick up the **cycle-only right turn** into Maysoule Road. Turn left into Wynter Street. At the railway follow the signed path for cyclists to the right. Do not cross the railway; turn right into Petergate and left into **Eltringham Street**.

3 Use the toucan crossing to reach the other side of York Road, then bear left to cross **Bridgend Road**. Follow the shared pavement round by McDonald's to go up Smugglers Way. Keep straight ahead along the Causeway, despite the unpromising signs. You will soon find yourself at **The Spit**, a new nature reserve created at the

MAP: OS Explorer 161 London South

START/FINISH: Rosary Gate, Battersea Park; grid ref: TQ286770

TRAILS/TRACKS: suburban streets

LANDSCAPE: parkland, suburban streetscape

PUBLIC TOILETS: Battersea Park

TOURIST INFORMATION: London Line, tel: 09068 663344

CYCLE HIRE: London Recumbents, Battersea Park, tel: 020 7498 6543

THE PUB: The Prince Albert, Battersea, SW11

🚫 Sections of this ride involve cycling in traffic; they may not be suitable for the youngest children

Getting to the start

Battersea Park's Rosary Gate is reached from Queenstown Road, north of the A3205 Battersea Park Road. There is a pay-and-display car park in Battersea Park.

Why do this cycle ride?

This ride is less picturesque than others in this book, but there is plenty of interest en route to make up for that. Battersea Park alone has enough to occupy a family for hours, while Putney is a pleasant place to spend time and watch the world go by. The Spit at Wandsworth Creek provides an opportunity to see how wildlife is being nurtured in the centre of the city.

Researched and written by: James Hatts

Battersea

LONDON

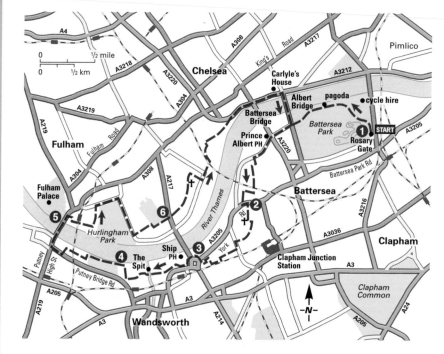

mouth of the River Wandle. Ride through the **industrial estate** to pick up Osiers Road. When this reaches the railway bridge at Point Pleasant turn right and head towards **the river**.

4 At the river pick up the well surfaced but **unsigned cycle track** and bear left. Soon you will reach the entrance to **Wandsworth Park**. It is necessary to dismount briefly as you leave the park to join Deodar Road. Keep straight ahead until the road bends to the left to join Putney Bridge Road. Bear right into **Putney High Street** and on to the bridge ahead.

5 Once over the bridge take the first right and follow **Ranelagh Gardens** under the railway viaduct. You need to skirt the perimeter of Hurlingham Park, so follow **Napier Avenue** to the left, turning right into Hurlingham Road at the north-western corner of the park. Head back south

towards the river along Broomhouse Road, but before the end take a left into Sulivan Road. Bear right into Peterborough Road, but almost immediately there is a left turn along a **segregated cycle track** along the bottom end of South Park.

6 Take care as you cross Wandsworth Bridge Road to pick up Stephenson Road on the other side. At the **Catholic church** bear right into Elswick Street. Turn right into Bagley's Lane at the end. At Townmead Road turn left and approach the **Chelsea Harbour complex**. Beyond the roundabout keep straight ahead and go under the railway, picking up Harbour Avenue on the other side. Turn left at the next roundabout, then bear right along Lots Road, past the former London Underground **power station**. Keep straight ahead when Lots Road joins Cheyne Walk. Return south using **Albert Bridge** and back to the start through the park via the outward route.

The Prince Albert

The Prince Albert stands opposite the Albert Gate to Battersea Park. This smart pub has been refurbished to a high standard and attracts a mixed clientele of locals and visitors to the park. The patio is tucked away behind the pub and offers ample seating, with large umbrellas and patio heaters for cooler days.

Food

The menu ranges from 'snacking plates' such as tomato and pesto bruschetta or savoury cheesecake to battered fish and fries or Jamaican jerk chicken. Rustic bread sandwiches with hot fillings in a rosemary and sea-salt pain-rustique are a popular choice. On Sundays a traditional roast lunch is served.

Family facilities

Children are welcome throughout the pub.

Alternative refreshment stops

There are cafés in Battersea Park and numerous pubs along the route, notably the Lots Road Pub & Dining Room.

☞ Where to go from here

Cross the Thames to Chelsea and take the children to the Chelsea World of Sport (www.chelseaworldofsport.com) on the Fulham Road. This interactive sports attraction has over 30 exhibits that will challenge visitors of all ages. There are 'interactive coaches' on hand to improve your performance and you can test your skill and compare yourself against the professionals at football, sprinting and volleyball. Just across Albert Bridge is Thomas Carlyle's House in Cheyne Row. This Queen Anne town house contains the historian and writer's books, portraits and personal relics, and has a lovely walled garden (www.nationaltrust.org.uk).

about the pub

The Prince Albert

85 Albert Bridge Road, Battersea
London SW11 4PF
Tel: 020 7228 0923
www.theprincealbert.com

DIRECTIONS: on the west side of the park, on the corner of Albert Bridge Road and Parkgate Road

PARKING: pay and display in Battersea Park, including at Rosary Gate and opposite the pub

OPEN: daily; all day

FOOD: daily; all day

BREWERY/COMPANY: free house

REAL ALE: changing guest beers

Along Regent's Canal

Explore the Regent's Canal
from the Thames to the
Islington Tunnel.

The Ragged School Museum and Angel Islington

The ride passes the Ragged School Museum, which is housed in three canalside warehouses, originally built to store lime juice and general provisions, but later used by Dr Barnardo to house the largest ragged school in London. The Museum was opened in 1990 to bring the unique history of this school to life. In a re-created classroom of the period you can experience how children in the Victorian East End were taught. Poor local children received a free education, breakfast, dinner and help finding their first job. The warehouses were used as a day school until 1908, and evening classes and Sunday schools continued until 1915.

The Angel Islington is instantly familiar to millions of people who have played the British version of the Monopoly board game. The area of Islington takes its name from an inn that once stood here. In the early 1800s it became a coaching inn; the first staging post outside the City of London. A local landmark, the inn was mentioned by Charles Dickens in *Oliver Twist*. The site of the pub is now occupied by a bank. Angel underground station boasts the longest escalators in Western Europe, with a vertical rise of 90ft (27m) and a length of 197ft (60m).

straight ahead; cycling is not permitted on the towpath here. At Colt Street turn left, then turn left again into Newell Street and follow it round to the right under the railway viaduct. **St Anne's Limehouse** is a striking landmark to the right.

the ride

1 Turn left along Narrow Street. At the entrance to **Limehouse Basin** continue

2 At the former **Limehouse Town Hall** use the toucan crossing to reach the other side of both Commercial Road and the Canal. Use the cycle lane to join Salmon Lane. At **Rhodeswell Street** the route

One of the many locks along the towpath

2h00 — **10 MILES** — **16.1 KM** — **LEVEL 123**

MAP: OS Explorer 173 London North

START/FINISH: Booty's Riverside Bar, Limehouse; grid ref: TQ360808

TRAILS/TRACKS: mostly surfaced towpath; some on-road sections

LANDSCAPE: urban waterside

PUBLIC TOILETS: scarce

TOURIST INFORMATION: Greenwich, tel: 0870 608 2000

CYCLE HIRE: Wharf Cycles, 21–23 Westferry Road, Docklands, E14 8JH, tel: 020 7987 2255

THE PUB: Booty's Riverside Bar, Limehouse

❶ Take care on narrow towpaths shared with pedestrians. A free permit is necessary to cycle along the Regent's Canal (www.waterscape.com)

Getting to the start

Booty's Riverside Bar is on Narrow Street, best approached from the east via Westferry Road. There is an underground car park at Westferry Circus (east of Narrow Street).

Why do this cycle ride?

This ride links the maritime history of London's Docklands with the urban sophistication of Islington. It makes use of the towpath of the Regent's Canal, opened in 1820 to link the Grand Union Canal's Paddington Arm with the River Thames. The towpath is an ideal route for cyclists to skirt the centre of London, free from traffic.

Researched and written by: James Hatts

---

continues straight ahead, leaving the traffic behind until Islington.

3 Don't take the footbridge over the canal, but turn right and use the ramp to join the towpath at **Salmon Lane Lock**. Follow the towpath under the railway and past the solitary remaining chimney. Ignore the National Cycle Network sign inviting you to head inland at Mile End Stadium and remain on the towpath. Just past the **Ben Jonson Road bridge** is the Ragged School

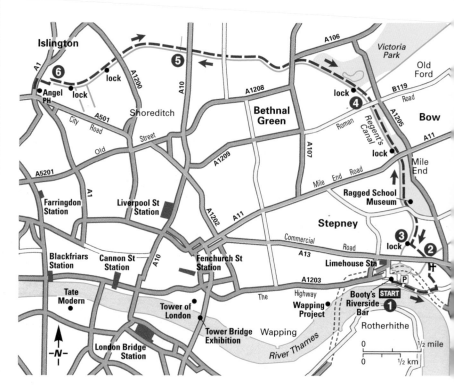

Museum's towpath café which you may be lucky enough to find open. The overhanging **warehouses** on the west side of the canal are a feature of this section. Beyond Mile End Lock look for the **water feature** on the right-hand side.

4 A bridge carries the towpath over the junction between the Regent's Canal and the Hertford Union Canal. Beyond **Old Ford Lock** there is some respite from the post-industrial landscape with a pleasantly green section alongside **Victoria Park**. Soon a **gasometer** looms ahead and the towpath passes under the road and railway.

5 The towpath then crosses a bridge over the entrance to Kingsland Basin. Beyond **Sturt's Lock** there are some larger permanently moored boats – these are converted Thames lighters that form part of the adjacent photographic studio complex. **City Road Basin** can be seen on the left, closely followed by City Road Lock. The entrance of **Islington Tunnel** soon looms.

6 Take the ramp up to road level. Head straight up **Duncan Street** to sample the attractions of The Angel Islington before tackling the return ride to Limehouse.

A sculpture in Mile End Park

Booty's Riverside Bar

Booty's Riverside Bar has been a pub since the late 1970s – the 18th-century building was once a barge-builders' store. Formerly known as the Waterman's Arms, it is now a mix between a traditional-style riverside pub and a wine bar, but has an atmosphere more akin to a friendly local pub. The single bar is long and narrow, with a lower level laid out for dining and with fine river views. Those who prefer to dine al fresco will have to settle for a table on the pavement side. There are bicycle racks directly opposite the bar.

Food

The menu offers steak and kidney pie, bangers and mash, a variety of ploughman's meals and much more; perhaps a delicious warming soup or a dressed crab salad. Desserts include apple pie and ice-cream.

Family facilities

Children are welcome inside the bar.

Alternative refreshment stops

There's a good canal-side café at the Ragged School Museum and a full range of refreshment opportunities at the Angel.

about the pub

Booty's Riverside Bar
94A Narrow Street, Limehouse
London E14 8PB
Tel: 020 7987 8343

DIRECTIONS: in Narrow Street, best approached from the east via Westferry Road
PARKING: on-street pay-and-display on Narrow Street
OPEN: daily; all day
FOOD: daily; all day
BREWERY/COMPANY: free house
REAL ALE: London Pride, Greene King IPA

☛ Where to go from here

Take a look at The Wapping Project, an international arts venue housed in a restored Grade II-listed hydraulic power station. You'll find contemporary gallery spaces, performance areas, a bookshop and a café. Head east along the Thames to visit the Tower Bridge Exhibition and learn more about how the world's famous bridge works and the history behind it. You can enjoy stunning views from the walkways situated 148ft (45m) above the Thames and visit the original Victorian turbines (www.towerbridge.org.uk).

From Bow to Walthamstow Marshes

Explore the Lee Navigation and East London's surprising open spaces.

Walthamstow Marshes

Walthamstow Marshes provide a haven for many types of wildlife not found elsewhere in Greater London. The marshland habitat sustains a breeding bird community including reed bunting, and reed, sedge and willow warblers. A variety of wintering birds visit the marshes and neighbouring reservoirs, and in autumn finches can be found feeding on the seeds of the tall herbs. Rare breed cattle, including longhorn, which have been reintroduced after an absence of more than 100 years, now graze the land. The cattle manage the vegetation, allowing creeping marshwort, which is only found at one other site, to thrive. Remains of pre-Viking boats have been found on the marshes, testimony to the early navigational importance of the

Lee. It was on Walthamstow Marshes that the first all-British powered flight was made by Alliott Verdon Roe in 1909. A blue plaque marks the railway arch where he assembled his triplane.

the ride

1 Start on the Tesco side of the bridge leading to **Three Mills Island** and look for the narrow entrance to the towpath heading north. Soon you reach a wide **quay**; head up the ramp just before the gas depot. Take care crossing the road under the Bow flyover. The path then crosses Bow Back River before returning to the towpath. At the railway bridge, the large building on the left is the **former Bryant & May match factory**. As you approach Old Ford Lock the Lee Navigation diverges from the course of the river; there is a very narrow gap for bicycles on the bridge which carries the path across the river. Rather than squeezing through the gap you may find it easier to use the stairs on the far side of the bridge where there is no such barrier.

2 At **Old Ford Lock** the former lockkeeper's house is well known as the home of Channel 4's cult 1990s morning show *The Big Breakfast*, and parts of the set can still be seen in the garden. Soon the junction with the **Hertford Union Canal** is reached. A series of road and railway bridges cross the Navigation in quick succession. Beyond the Homerton Road bridge the Navigation runs alongside **Hackney Marsh,** and the route for cyclists leaves the towpath to run on the inland side of the fence. Just past the **white gate** across the track return to the towpath.

2h00 — **8.5 MILES** — **13.7 KM** — **LEVEL 1**23

MAP: OS Explorer 162 Greenwich & Gravesend and 173 Epping Forest and Lee Valley

START/FINISH: Three Mills, Bow; grid ref: SK241515

TRAILS/TRACKS: mixed; some surfaced paths, some gravel tracks

LANDSCAPE: waterside, marsh and parkland

PUBLIC TOILETS: at Springfield Park

TOURIST INFORMATION: Greenwich, tel: 0870 608 2000

CYCLE HIRE: none locally

THE PUB: The Kings Arms, Bow, E3

❶ One major road crossing

Getting to the start

Three Mills Island can be reached via Hancock Road from the Bow Interchange where the A11 meets the A12 Blackwall Tunnel Northern Approach. Follow signs to Tesco Superstore, south of the A11/A118 interchange. You can use the Tesco car park.

Why do this cycle ride?

This is an enjoyable circuit linking many points of interest in the Lower Lee Valley. From the industrial history of Three Mills to 1990s television nostalgia and the first all-British powered flight, this ride has it all.

Researched and written by: James Hatts

3 A long brick wall marks the edge of the **Middlesex Filter Beds Nature Reserve**. At the bridge the towpath moves to the west bank. Past the Princess of Wales pub there is a rough section of path under the bridge. It then skirts the edge of **North Millfields Recreation Ground**. The navigation is bordered by housing to the west and **Walthamstow Marshes** to the east. Beyond the railway bridge and the Anchor and Hope pub is Springfield Park. The route heads inland to pass the **adventure playground**.

4 At the bottom of Spring Hill there is a useful waterside café. Cross the bridge here to reach **Springfield Marina**, and continue straight ahead with Warwick Reservoir on your left and the marina on your right. At the vehicle entrance to the marina, stay on the surfaced roadway; look for the painted **bicycle symbol**. Mind your head as you pass underneath the low railway bridge. Turn right immediately through the gate into the playing field. The undulating gravel track enjoys some excellent views.

5 Soon the track scoops down under the railway junction and emerges on to a wide causeway. The **Lea Bridge Riding School** is to the left. The left-hand tunnel under the Lea Bridge Road is for cyclists.

Top: Three Mills
Left: Hackney Marshes

B o w

LONDON

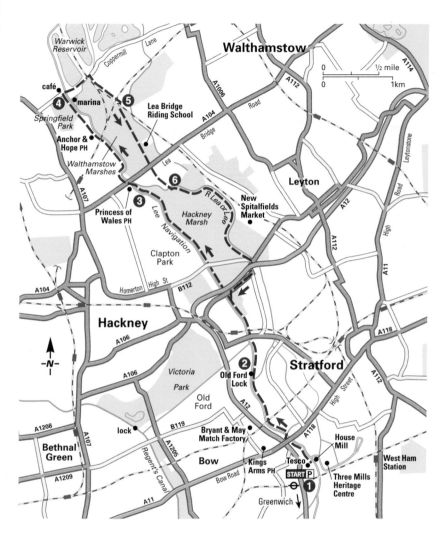

Follow the path through the filter beds. A distinctive **red bridge** carries the path across the River Lee and on to Hackney Marsh.

6 Once across the bridge, turn left and follow the tree-lined **riverside path**. This section features a 'trim trail' of fitness equipment. There are views of the Temple Mills railway depot and New Spitalfields Market. At the bridge linking the marsh with the recreation ground across the river,

continue straight ahead. When the path emerges on to Homerton Road, use the toucan crossing. Pass under the flyover and turn right along **Eastway**, using the cycle lane on the pavement. Continue past the service station. Just before the bridge across the Navigation keep your eyes peeled for a **blue squeeze-gate**, which provides access to the towpath. On joining the towpath, turn left and return to **Three Mills** via the outward route.

The Kings Arms

about the pub

The Kings Arms
167 Bow Road, Bow
London E3 2SG
Tel: 020 8981 1398

DIRECTIONS: on the A11 close to Bow
Church. To reach it from Three Mills follow
the route to Bow Flyover, cross the road and
turn left up the hill past the church

PARKING: there is no parking close to
the pub

OPEN: daily; all day

FOOD: no food Saturday lunchtime and
Sunday evening

BREWERY/COMPANY: free house

REAL ALE: none served

*The Kings Arms is a traditional East End
pub and attracts a predominantly local
clientele. This is not the smartest or
most modern of pubs, but is ideal for
a reasonably priced Thai meal and a
drink before or after tackling your ride.
The historic church of St Mary's Bow –
sometimes known as Bow Church – is
on an island in the middle of the road
just across from the pub. There are
some seats on the wide pavement
outside. Cycle racks are also available
right outside the pub.*

Food

Thai cuisine is the culinary attraction.
Starters range from chicken wings in
garlic sauce to tofu surprise. Main courses
include curries and stir-fry dishes, and
there's deep-fried ice-cream for dessert.
On Sunday afternoons a traditional roast
lunch is served, with a limited selection
from the Thai menu available.

Family facilities

Although there are no special facilities for
children they are welcome inside the pub.

Alternative refreshment stops

Try the café at Springfield Marina or one
of the riverside pubs.

☞ Where to go from here

Three Mills Island boasts hundreds of years
of industrial heritage and the House Mill is
Britain's oldest and largest restored tidal
mill, built in 1776. Together with the Clock
Mill, re-built in 1817, they are two of the
most elegant waterside buildings in
London. You can tour the House Mill on
Sundays between May and September.
There are also trips on East London's canals
from here (www.leevalleypark.org.uk).

East from Greenwich along the Thames

Explore the Millennium Dome, the Thames Barrier and Royal Arsenal.

Thames Barrier and Royal Arsenal

The Thames Barrier has been put to use more than 80 times to protect London from flooding. Construction began in 1974 and a decade later the Queen carried out the official opening. More than 80 staff are required to operate and maintain the flood defences. The barrier is made up of ten movable gates positioned end-to-end across the river. It's closed once a month for testing and maintenance; dates are published on the Environment Agency's website. The Agency estimates that a major flood in central London could cost as much as £30,000 million.

The first ordnance stores at Woolwich were set up in the 16th century by Henry VIII, when gun manufacturing was moved from the City of London to the comparative safety of Woolwich. From the early 1700s Woolwich became the headquarters of the Royal Artillery companies, and a military academy was established soon after. The title Royal Arsenal was granted in 1805 by George III, in recognition of Woolwich's

Across the Thames is the Millennium Dome

importance in ordnance manufacturing. The Royal Ordnance Factory closed in 1967 with the loss of thousands of jobs. The site has now been restored and regenerated into an attractive riverside leisure complex.

the ride

1 If you are starting from the parking at **Cutty Sark Gardens** wheel your bike along the riverside walk to the **Cutty Sark** pub and turn right along Ballast Quay, then bear right into Pelton Road. At the Royal Standard pub turn left into Christchurch Way. As you approach the entrance to the **Alcatel complex,** turn right into Mauritius Road. On reaching Blackwall Lane turn left into the bus lane. Just before the traffic lights take the **cycle path** on the left which runs along the pavement of Tunnel Avenue. At the footbridge look for the **green surfaced track** on the left.

2 Cross the footbridge and turn left into Boord Street. At **Millennium Way,** join the cycle path directly ahead. At West Parkside continue straight on and when you reach the riverside, turn right. Just past the colourful buildings of Greenwich Millennium Village you will reach the **Greenwich Peninsula Ecology Park**.

3 The outer boardwalk is open at all times and considerate cyclists are welcome. Continue along the riverside path, which turns inland to skirt the **Greenwich Yacht Club**'s fenced enclosure. Remain on the riverside past the aggregate recycling works. At the end of that section, stay on the street called **Riverside**, with the large Sainsbury's depot to your right. Look out for

MAP: OS Explorer 162 Greenwich & Gravesend

START/FINISH: Cutty Sark pub, Ballast Quay; grid ref: TQ389782. Pay parking at Cutty Sark Gardens

TRAILS/TRACKS: largely surfaced cycle lanes, some cobbled streets

LANDSCAPE: industrial and waterside

PUBLIC TOILETS: close to Woolwich Ferry

TOURIST INFORMATION: Greenwich, tel: 0870 608 2000

CYCLE HIRE: none locally

THE PUB: Cutty Sark, Greenwich, SE10

! This ride includes some busy on-road sections where you may prefer to dismount

Getting to the start

The Cutty Sark pub is north east of Greenwich town centre. Lassell Street leads to Ballast Quay from Trafalgar Road (A206). On-street metered parking is limited to 2 hours; Greenwich Council underground parking at Cutty Sark Gardens is a short walk or ride.

Why do this cycle ride?

In the space of just 3 miles (4.8km) of riverside there is at least a millennium's worth of London's industrial, military and seafaring heritage to explore, from Maritime Greenwich to the Royal Arsenal, via the engineering feat of the Thames Barrier and the unmistakable landmark of the Millennium Dome.

Researched and written by: James Hatts

Greenwich LONDON

the remains of old dockside railway tracks on your left. At **Anchor and Hope Lane** take the off-road path straight ahead.

4 On reaching the **Thames Barrier**, the green-surfaced route around the complex is well-signed and easy to follow. At the former Thames Barrier Arms pub, go straight ahead along the narrow and slightly overgrown path. There is a steep slope up to the crossing at **Woolwich Church Street**. Turn left along the road here. When you reach the roundabout, take the second exit (Ruston Road). Look for the left turn where Ruston Road heads towards the river. Turn left here and left again at **Harlinger Road**. At the T-junction turn right, then right again.

5 A sign asks cyclists to dismount for the 40yd (37m) section between the road and the riverside. When you rejoin the riverside opposite the **Tate & Lyle works**

on the north bank, turn right. When the pedestrian route uses steps to cross a wall, the cycle path heads inland where there is a ramp and returns to the **riverside**.

6 At the canons on the riverside turn inland past the **Clockhouse Community Centre**. At Leda Road make your way up the slope to join Woolwich Church Street. You may prefer to dismount and push your bike to reach the **Woolwich Free Ferry**. At the Ferry Approach look for the cycle signs by the ambulance station. Pass the Waterfront Leisure Centre and the entrance to the **Woolwich Foot Tunnel**. Continue along the riverside to **Royal Arsenal Pier**, where a large piazza provides access to the revitalised Royal Arsenal complex, including the Firepower Museum. From here it is possible to cycle inland to the shops and services of Woolwich town centre before you return to **Greenwich**.

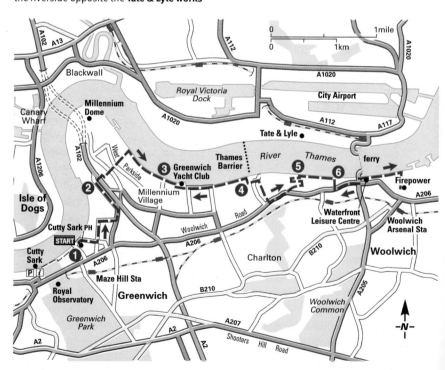

The Cutty Sark Tavern

Originally the Union Tavern, this 1695 waterside pub was renamed when the world-famous tea-clipper was dry-docked upriver in 1954. It is part of an attractive row of historic buildings surrounded by modern developments. Inside you will find low beams, creaking floorboards, dark panelling and, from large bow windows in the upstairs bar, commanding views of the Thames, the clusters of skyscrapers at Canary Wharf and the unmistakable Millennium Dome. There is splendid riverside seating on the waterside terrace across the narrow cobbled street.

Food

A permanent menu of door-step sandwiches and jacket potatoes is backed up with daily specials such as chicken breast stuffed with Brie, feta cheese and olive salad. A separate board lists fish and seafood dishes such as lemon pepper tiger prawns with rice and salad, chilli smoked salmon and mussels. Desserts include chocolate fudge cake and apple pie. Sunday roast lunches are also available.

Family facilities

Children are welcome inside the pub. The riverside terrace is also ideal for families.

Alternative refreshment stops

There is a terrace café at the Thames Barrier and a café at the Royal Arsenal.

☛ Where to go from here

Step on board the Cutty Sark, the fastest tea clipper ever; built in 1869, she once sailed 363 miles (584km) in a single day (www.cuttysark.org.uk). Put science into action with touch-screen displays and be awed by the big guns at Firepower – the Royal Artillery Museum, where the history of artillery from stone shot to shell is explained (www.firepower.org.uk). At the Thames Barrier Learning and Information Centre find out more about the world's largest movable flood barrier, the flood threat of the Thames and the construction of this £535 million project (www.environment-agency.gov.uk).

Greenwich LONDON

about the pub

The Cutty Sark Tavern
4–7 Ballast Quay, Greenwich
London SE10 9PD
Tel: 020 8858 3146

DIRECTIONS:	see Getting to the start
PARKING:	metered roadside parking
OPEN:	daily; all day
FOOD:	daily; all day (until 6pm at weekends)
BREWERY/COMPANY:	free house
REAL ALE:	Fuller's London Pride, Greene King Old Speckled Hen, Adnams Broadside

Acknowledgements

The Automobile Association would like to thank the following photographers, companies and picture libraries for their assistance in the preparation of this book.

Abbreviations for the picture credits are as follows: - (t) top; (b) bottom; (l) left; (r) right; (AA) AA World Travel Library.

Front cover AA/J Miller; Back cover AA/N Setchfield; 3 AA/J Miller; 6/7 AA/J Miller; 7b AA/R Mort; 12 AA/W Voysey; 13 AA/W Voysey; 15 AA/D Foster; 18 AA/J O'Carroll; 19 AA/W Voysey; 20/21 AA/T Souter; 23 AA/W Voysey; 25 AA/W Voysey; 26 AA/W Voysey; 27 AA/D Foster; 28 AA/T Locke; 29t AA/T Locke; 31 AA/T Locke; 33 AA/T Souter; 34 AA/J Miller; 35 AA/T Locke; 37 AA/T Locke; 39 AA/T Locke; 40/41 AA/T Locke; 43 AA/T Locke; 44b AA/T Locke; 44/45t AA/M Trelawny; 47 AA/T Locke; 49 AA/T Locke; 51 AA/P Toms; 54 AA; 55 AA/T Locke; 56 AA/D Noble; 59 AA/T Locke; 60/61 AA/J Hatts; 62 AA/J Hatts; 63 AA/J Hatts; 64/65 AA/J Hatts; 65b AA/M Trelawny; 67 AA/J Hatts; 68 AA/J Hatts; 69 AA/J Hatts; 71 AA/J Hatts; 72/73 AA/J Hatts; 73t AA/J Hatts; 75 AA/J Hatts; 76/77 AA/R Mort; 79 AA/J Hatts; 80 AA/J Hatts; 81 AA/J Hatts; 83 AA/J Hatts; 84 AA/J Hatts; 85 AA/J Hatts; 87 AA/J Hatts; 88/89 AA/J Hatts; 91 AA/ J Hatts; 92/93 AA/J Hatts; 94 AA/S McBride; 95 AA/J Hatts; 96 AA/J Hatts; 97 AA/L Hatts; 99 AA/J Hatts; 100/101 AA/J Hatts; 102 AA/J Hatts; 103 AA/J Hatts; 104 AA/J Hatts; 105 AA/J Hatts; 107 AA/J Hatts; 108 AA/L/ Hatts; 111 AA/J Hatts

Every effort has been made to trace the copyright holders, and we apologise in advance for any accidental errors. We would be happy to apply the corrections in the following edition of this publication.